Book Two From the Out of the Blue and into My Heart series...

I0161726

LET NO
JOY GO
UNCLAIMED

The Blessings Continue

"*Loving and guiding, Poetic in nature, His words bless and keep me whole*"

-Daniel Ethan Lowe

MIKE STEFFKE

Let No Joy Go Unclaimed
– The Blessings Continue
By Mike Steffke

Printed in the USA

ISBN 978-0-999-7560-4-1

Acknowledgments

A heartfelt thank you to all who read and supported my first book in this series. Your encouragement and interest are deeply appreciated.

Thank you so much!

To my loving wife Debi;

Thank you for your input, and feedback! Your involvement and supportive words inspire me to seek my passion to write from the heart!

Preface

A couple years back I set out to write a series of short stories, to illustrate how the Love of Jesus graciously guides us when life is Christ centered. After reading a few of my early efforts to my wife Debi, she suggested I focus my story writing on the life of one specific character. Her wonderful idea changed everything, and one inspiring story after another flowed out of my pencil. Yes, I am old school; I write with pencil in a composition book. The finished product became the life story of a character I created named Daniel Ethan Lowe.

While writing about Daniel's life, I felt the Lord's presence, inspiring me in ways I'd never experienced. Hours passed like minutes; I only stopped to sharpen my group of seven pencils.

As my chapters grew in numbers, I soon discovered Daniel's amazing life experiences could not be covered in one book. The chapters to follow detail the blessings of the incredible events Daniel witnessed, as his life continues.

This entire writing experience has been life changing. My purpose in publishing, is to share the inspiration which the Lord places on my heart. My hope is you will similarly be touched and encouraged by His presence while reading.

Enjoy Daniel's journey, as he continues to elate in the greatest gift one can receive; the gift of life.

Blessings to all,

Mike Steffke

Introduction

This is the continuing story of Daniel Ethan Lowe. Every morning Daniel gives thanks for the opportunity to relish the gift of a new day. He remains grateful for the people who share life with him; his loving family and dear friends. All of these amazing people fondly touch Daniel's heart in a special way, as he and Jesus journey through life with them.

Now in his forties, as Daniel continues to receive Jesus's gracious poetic guidance, he fondly shares memorable life changing episodes of his fruitful life.

Often with a touch of humor, but always in appreciation of life's blessings, journey with Daniel in his growth and elation as he, his wife Kelly Lynn, and children Dana and Brandon, seek to **Let no joy go unclaimed!**

Blessings to all, Mike Steffke.

Table of Contents

Going forward from the author

Preciously Published Works

Age 41

Reunion; Forty Something Style

1988

Just yesterday I was on the phone with my college friend and music store owner, Willis Epps. The exchange of back and forth banter was like the old days, as we chatted and caught up. After proudly discussing our children's latest endeavors, our conversation turned to life in our forties. "Let's not forget my ole' friend, at 41 we're still young. I see many exciting adventures ahead to discover and enjoy", I optimistically stated. "I'm still able to shoot a respectable round of golf, and competitively play the occasional soft ball game", I proudly cited. "Maybe so, but stretching a single into a double via the head first slide is no longer on the table", Willis cautiously countered. How true; we chuckled and commiserated how our bodies brutally remind us many of our past talents are pleasant but distant memories. With that sobering thought agreed upon, we decided to chat more often and get together soon. After my talk with Willis, I resigned to a fact I've been ignoring for the past five years. I actually verbalize the point aloud to let it sink in... *I no longer can do everything I did as a younger adult.*

I am now entering my marvelous mid-term of mortality; ages 41-49 in the life cycle. After my forties (should the Good Lord be willing), I'll begin my second half of joy on Earth. If I want to thrive throughout those years to come, I'll need to elevate my game to maintain a *healthy temple*. If I revitalize the body now, healthy dividends will be received, allowing me to stay physically vibrant going forward. Otherwise, if I don't have a good handle on things; the *temple walls* may begin to crumble to the ground.

Speaking of physical activity, over this past weekend, we hiked one of the many picturesque and inspiring mountain trails in the western Carolinas. The physical demands were challenging but the breathtaking scenery the Lord provided fueled my energy enabling me to keep up with the kids and Kelly. Note; I said the kids and Kelly. True she is right behind me at 40, but she's as fit as she was at 30, and just as energetic. Her conditioning alone should encourage me to raise the bar, and strive to be as healthy as I can.

Okay, I've drawn the line in the sand, I want to live healthier and maintain my vitality. So, what's my go forward plan to keep fit? We all know the basics; exercise, work out, eat right, limit the sweets, I understand the drill, but how do I make this a sustainable plan? How do I keep my interests up to stay involved with the program? I don't want to be stuck in a gym, toiling on a stationary bike or a tread mill; one word for that approach, boring! I could start running again as I did in Toledo, minus the pit stop at Vinni's Pizza afterwards. I could join an over 40 softball league. I love playing, but standing around while in the field and waiting for my turn to hit, hardly seem like effective physical conditioning. What then? When in doubt go down the proven avenue of success, and consult with one who bears great knowledge in this realm; Kelly Lynn.

Kelly has been blessed with excellent genes. She maintains a great workout ethic which keeps her in splendid condition, and allows her to look impressive in her jeans. She loves a good cardio workout; eats lots of salad, and limits soft drinks and dessert to special occasions only. I find that type of training a bit less thrilling than Kelly. I also have a far less desirable history of proper eating habits. I've cut out most fast foods, but never been one to pass up dessert or eat the last piece of pizza, even if it sits in the fridge for a day or two. I need to get serious; now is the time for Kelly and me to hash out a plan to make sure we're both prepared for our next forty or so years, should we be so blessed.

The next day upon arriving home from the nursery, I open the front door to receive my welcome home greeting from our fur baby, Dee. My next normal inclination is to take a big whiff and see what Kelly has in store for dinner. With my sense of smell elevated, I eagerly inhale to determine what's on the menu, but I come up blank! No fantastic aroma billowing from the kitchen; not a savory scent of beef roast, no soothing sound of chicken sizzling in the pan, and certainly no aromatic trail of seafood to be had. Nothing! Perhaps Kelly is looking to go out for a mid-week meal, seeking a respite from the rigors of her culinary skills? I settled on that conclusion, clearly the kitchen is getting the night off.

"I'm in the kitchen hon. C'mon in and check out what we're having' for dinner", my sweet loving wife suggested. As I near the kitchen, I continue to take a sniff with each advancing step, but still no clue as to what is on the menu. "Here it is Dan", Kelly announced while putting the finishing touches on our dinner. Before my eyes sat the most impressive salad I had ever seen. The leafy creation stood tall and proud, delightfully poised in Kelly's largest stainless-steel bowl. Romaine lettuce, iceberg lettuce, baby spinach leaves, kale, cut carrots, chopped celery, grape tomatoes, sliced eggs, and some bits of ham (emphasis on bits) all covered in a light coating of mozzarella cheese. Wow, she must have picked the garden clean! "My super chef's salad", Kelly proudly announced. "Looks great dear, quite a large appetizer", I quipped still holding out for something a bit meatier. "Nope this is it, everything we need in one bowl, lean, lots of vitamins, low in carbohydrates, and a great taste. We'll top it with a vinegar and light oil dressing", Kelly said while taking a seat.

Again, I am reminded I am one of the most blessed men to ever live. After saying grace, before me is a complete and healthy dinner. Along with this balanced meal, I'll share enjoyable, sparkling conversation with a charming, intelligent, and lovely lady. Amazingly, one simple mention of improving my diet and beginning an exercise plan, and I'm eating more sensibly and soon to enjoy an after-dinner stroll for good measure.

Upon finishing our salads, we let the meal settle for a few minutes than set out for our evening walk. Despite spending much of the day on my feet at the nursery, I've discovered a new found energy after eating my vitamin laden meal. While taking in the picture-perfect evening, the addictive conversation and encouragement from my walking partner made the venture that much more pleasurable. Jesus guided us up and down the streets, enabling us to cross paths with dear neighbors, and friendly people around every turn.

Once home, my wife suggested other exercise ideas and voiced a few new dishes she would like to try, to add some variety to our fitness effort. Make no mistake, Kelly likes pizza, cake and pie with the best of them, but she learned long ago these foods are treats and not staples.

By bed time I was whipped. After a full day of renting and selling the big toys (construction equipment) and strolling up and down our neighborhood streets, I was ready to journal, then close in prayer and thanks for a pleasurable day. This was a day of enlightenment, and confirmation there are always new things to try and appreciate. But Jesus wasn't done with me quite yet; He shared these thoughts after lights out...

I am your food
Your life I fill
Partake from My garden
Trust in My Will

I strengthen your body
I encourage your growth
To seek other ventures
As I mentor you both

I am your food
Pursue righteous deeds
Gather the herd
Let hearts intercede

In fellowship walk
Greet all My kin
As you smile and talk
Your decade begins

Upon this new day, I stretched and broadly smiled. I was relishing the joy of receiving the latest edition of encouraging and mentoring words from Jesus. But no time to do a full evaluation on the dream now, it's Friday and the nursery starts early; it's always busy going into the weekend.

The rental equipment is swiftly leaving the shop and the customers are loading their trucks with mulch, dirt and yard fixtures. The day is flying by but I keep going back to my dream last night. The Lord clearly reminded me He is my source of nourishment and strength. I also heard I will be gathering with people, and greeting them in some yet to be disclosed way. This notion has my curiosity swirling.

After dinner (baked tilapia and sweet potatoes) we set out for our evening stroll. I shared with Kelly some of the conversation I had with Willis earlier in the week. She and I spoke about our life together as a couple and our precious friends, who have impacted our lives over the years. We brought up name after name of people that have touched us in a positive way. Our old friends from Ohio like Alex Snow, Barton Lake, Jenny Masters, and Pete and Denise Blair. Friends in the Carolinas like Dave and Cindy Langley and Willis's brother Melvin. Kelly and I soon realized too much time had elapsed since seeing many of them. Also, though not too surprisingly, with the exception of Pete Blair who recently hit the big 5-0, all of us are in our forties. The solution in renewing these long overdue relationships became obvious; a reunion of old friends. All of our dear forty somethings need to gather in one festive occasion. Most of them know one another in some capacity through weddings and birthdays, so they are not strangers to one another. "That's it, we need to plan a reunion, Kelly", I suggested. "Exactly Dan, what a great idea; a big gathering of our brethren in celebration of life together over the years. We'll include Ron and Daryl too," Kelly said in closing.

Over the next several days, we had contacted and got about a dozen out of town people able to celebrate with us. Next month Kelly, me and good friend and business partner Dave Langley will be hosting the *reunion of forty somethings*. Everyone will stay with either us, the Langley's or with Willis. Kelly and I will host the Friday kickoff event and the main day will be graciously hosted at Dave and Cindy's inviting and spacious lake front home.

The reunion weekend is here. Kelly, me, the Langley's, and the Epps guys are about to receive the first of the out of town guests. Barton, Alex, and their wives, along with Ron and Sandy all flew in together from Ohio. Daryl and Sherry came in next. Jenny Masters and husband

Ben drove in from Cleveland, and finally Pete and Cindy Blair arrived, completing the out of town contingent.

That evening after a rousing game of plastic bat and ball, we assembled on our outdoor patio and deck to break bread as one blessed group of forty-year old's. By the way, I managed to stretch a single into a double without the need for a head first slide. My effort earned a big smile and a thumbs up from Willis. It also helped that the bases were only forty feet apart. Speaking of Willis, he and Kelly teamed up early in the day preparing our delicious meal for day one. Barbequed pulled pork and a huge beef brisket, have been biding their time in the smoker since mid-morning. Carolina coleslaw, potato salad, and green beans complete the menu. Melvin Epps brought a huge peach cobbler and Kelly baked six dozen chocolate chip coconut cookies. The *temple* is going to take a massive hit this weekend.

After grace and gorging on the fabulous spread the guys and Kelly prepared, we shared one glorious story after another recalling the old days. We then took some group pictures to further capture the memory of this splendid gathering. We decided to sprawl out on the lawn in World Series championship style. We took several shots; some of us struck silly poses, others knelt, or sat arm in arm. Kelly and I were in total awe over the fun we were having, while reminiscing with some of God's dearest creations.

As the evening came to a close and everyone began to disperse, we clutched on to one another as long as we could, while saying our goodbyes. Fortunately for this special group... we can do it all over again tomorrow!

Day two at the Langley's was awesome. Badminton, board games, fishing off the dock, and trips around the lake on Dave's boat, were just some of the wonderful happenings. Some of the guys wanted to create a human pyramid, but after a few lackluster attempts, age reared its cruel head and nixed the idea. We all had a good laugh citing our common sense likely prevented potential injury. Again, it was food galore at the Langley's... burgers, dogs, brats, and ribs. Cindy Langley made a huge salad, dwarfing the creation Kelly made when I started my diet program. Speaking of which, before the reunion weekend I had already dropped 8 pounds, and felt my energy levels climbing every day. I decided to refrain from weighing myself after the weekend, and chance closing this glorious event on an unpleasing note.

Day three was held at a pavilion in our city park. Willis presided over a heartfelt and moving outdoor Sunday service. Melvin closed our gathering with an inspirational and touching prayer, and then asked for travel mercies for our dear friends. We served sausage sandwiches, bagels, juice and coffee to all for breakfast.

Soon everyone said their goodbyes together, as they made their way back to the airport or hit the highway.

That evening Kelly and I agreed this was one of the best weekends we ever experienced together. Why not, we have been blessed with the Lord's best since Friday.

Looking back, as I journaled Sunday night before bed, I went back to my last dream poem from Jesus. As the poem said, He is our food and He sustained all of us. We gathered the herd and we greeted one another with happy hearts. He guided all of us and no one was hurt or injured during our escapades. He also blessed every one of us in a special way. Each person will take that blessing home to cherish forever. Finally, as the last line of the poem states, *Your decade begins.* Indeed, it does, and what a glorious time we all had starting it together.

Age 42

A Chance at My Dream Car

1989

Let's have a little chat about cars. Those vigorous vehicles designed to get us from point A to point B. Those cherished chariots of conveyance. Those motorized marvels of maneuverability. Our cars seem to be an extension of our personalities, and the choice of rides covers the gamut to satisfy every discernable taste, in an assortment of colors spilling off a pallet of endless choices.

Despite this boundless array of possibilities, my conservative, dare I say boring choice of vehicle ownership has always looked past the sleeker models and gravitated to traditional makes and styles. I'm a person of comfort, one who tends to lean toward the roominess, and the customary seating space of a full-sized ride. So how does a traditional person as myself, seemingly overnight entertain the thought of buying a 1989 Chevrolet Corvette, T top convertible, 5.7 LT engine, with 240 horsepower?

On a whim, I stopped at a Cheve dealership and with little coaxing, I took a seat in one of these prized babies. It had to be the excitement of the moment, but it just felt so good. By the way, this machine can go 175 MPH! Granted I don't plan a trip to the Auto Baum any time soon, but I have to tell you, this thing has really grabbed my eye. Blue Metallic in color; five spoke aluminum wheels, heated side mirrors, a Bose sound system, the works! Perhaps I'm trying to justify this potential purchase, as kind of a mid-career reward? I'm trying to wrap my mind around why I would even be considering a car like this. Did I mention it can go 175 MHP?

As noted, my car selection is traditional and predictable. Yes, I'm conservative, even dull when it comes to vehicle choice, but I have never thought of myself as a cool car guy. My choice of conservative vehicle ownership is twofold; I've never felt the desire to excite total strangers with an impressive vehicle, as we pass one another going to and from work. Also, a super stylish ride sitting in my driveway has simply never appeared on my bucket list. That's just me. Besides, since I am in the industrial tool/ nursery business, though I have a full-sized Buick at home, I found a proven reliable pickup truck properly fits my daily vehicle needs. At times, I may decide to personally deliver tools or industrial products to the customer, if I feel it is necessary.   Since many of those deliveries would be challenging in my Buick La Sabre, a well-maintained nice-looking work truck does it for me.

At home, Kelly too needs space in her vehicle. If she had her druthers, another pickup truck would suit her just fine. She loves the freedom of buying an oversized item and having the ability of getting it loaded up and trucked home curtesy of her wheel skills. Bags of mulch or dirt, as she ventures out to the nursery, often are regular passengers of hers. That brings us up to her present vehicle, a Ford Aerostar with large side windows. However, on a more personal note, Kelly has other reasons for driving a vehicle with generous cargo space.

Shifting gears, (pun intended) allow me a moment to take a deep breath, gather myself, and share with you something on a more somber note. Sadly, my dear Kelly has a serious problem; more accurately put she has an addiction. This intolerant disorder is one which she has suffered from in private, for many years.   To make matters worse, she is in denial this condition is even a problem. That being said, I doubt she will be successful in defeating this awful affliction. A habit so addictive it ruthlessly controls one's entire weekend existence... Kelly is a garage sale junkie!

This compulsive, unforgiving disorder is so controlling; it will run through your "mad money" so quickly, you'll never know what hit you. The habitual thrill of the buy is so intense, so obsessive, it entices a woman to rise at 5:30 AM, put on jeans and a baseball cap and blow out of the house, often without the boost provided by a cup of morning joe. The soothing morning shower, not a chance, makeup, forget it, there are sales to be had! After all, how can you possibly survive a weekend, without attempting to spend perfectly good money on something that is one step away from being put to the curb? Not only that, time is not on your side. Most of these sales frenzies set up at dawn and close up shop before noon, 1:00 PM if you are lucky. Once they pack up, you'll need to survive on whatever pleasure you derived from your buying fix, until these merciless dealers resurface on the following weekend.

This past Saturday, Kelly again got her fix and made the buy of the day, which this time required my assistance to seal the deal. It seems she spotted and bought a large table and six chairs, the likes of which would not easily fit into her vehicle. She managed to enlist the services of two young men who helped her carry the table to the corner. At this point she called me and before I knew it, I was an accomplice en route to dismantle this four-legged monster. The plan was to disassemble the beast, piece it into her vehicle, then load the remaining loot into my truck.

While in route and despite the ever present "what were you thinking" racing in my head, I must admit, Kelly has a keen eye for scoping out the choicest pieces of garage sale inventory. She is blessed with the ability to seek out a quality piece of furniture, assess the workmanship (even the maker in some cases) with one eye, and hone in on a parking spot with the other.

Once I arrived on scene and performed my curbside surgery, the disassembled booty was loaded up. We head back to our garage to reassemble and figure out where this thing could possibly go. I have only one thing to say about my lovely garage sale junkie; please pray for her recovery, and that she will be guided through this darkness.

I say all of this tongue in cheek, given my dear Kelly is one of the most generous people on the planet. This table and chair unit is a quality set, and will be greatly appreciated by a young couple who attends our church. Tia and Brett Gaines recently married and bought a new little home close to our church. Unfortunately, on move in day Brett was involved in a rear end collision, which included several cars. Thankfully, no one was seriously hurt, but the trailer Ben was pulling took quite a hit and much of their furniture was damage beyond use. Their dining room set was amongst the causalities, and basically was reduced to kindling. Thanks to Kelly's giving heart, a place to break bread will become one less concern for this young family. This deserving couple will receive great elation in accepting this beautiful table, but the joy will be as much claimed by Kelly. My generous wife continues to be a blessing to anyone fortunate enough to know her!

But discussion regarding Kelly and her garage sale prowess, led me away from the topic of considering the new Vette.   Let's dissect this problem down to manageable facts, if it's even a problem. Financially we are doing well, our home is nearly paid for, 401K's are trending nicely and the economy is expected to do well, perhaps boom in the next decade. Everything seems to be in place to pull the trigger on the purchase. Even Kelly is supportive and is leaving the decision entirely up to me, providing this is what I really want. In her words, "you have been a very generous provider over the years; reward yourself with something special". While Kelly made that statement with an honest heart, she is also a superb negotiator. She knows her support will garner a fair amount of seat time in the Vette, given she signed off to go forward with the buy.   The usual stumbling block of resistance normally would come from one's better half, but that is simply not the case here. It seems like all systems are go.   Nevertheless, being a conservative thinker, I must consider any and all pitfalls. I decided to sleep on it and take it to Jesus in prayer. I truly do not expect the Lord to suggest a definitive yea or nay. He won't force us to do anything. He simply offers His words and He allow us the freedom of deciding. Perhaps, I'm overthinking the whole thing since this is my chance to receive a special want of mine. Yet I know there are wants and there are needs in this world, and needs must be satisfied first. Maybe it's just me, but I'm finding it difficult to place the word *need* and the word *Corvette*, in the same sentence.

For a week or so I put the purchase of the Vette on the back burner, but the notion rekindled each time I passed the dealership as I commuted to and from work. Every night during prayers of thanks for family, friends, and the joys of the day, I would ask for guidance on the car, before dropping off into dreamland. Finally, during one of my rest laden sweet dreams, I once again found myself sharing a park bench with the spirit of Jesus. This time we were gently swinging, and comfortably seated under a sea of golden yellow and red leaves, peacefully falling from the trees above. The sound of the leaves landing on the bench and ground was the only audible sound. At that point the beautiful refrains of Jesus filled my heart...

As questions linger
Do they align?
Voice your request
Let truth define
To seek the reason
Of what you yearn
To harness the season
As questions burn

Doubt has loomed
From the very start
One can't decide
With a blissful heart
There is no call
From deep within
To ease the fall
Of reasons thin

Stylish and blue
Sleek and refined
Does accord ring true
To ease your mind?
No trumpet is sounded
To rally the heart
Just thoughts unfounded
Soon to part

Wow! That's it? This is my morning thought? What was it I ate just before bed? Yes, while it was poetic in nature, the content was stark, fragmented, and rather unsettling. I'm not at all receiving the positive start to a new day, or any blissful thought about the Vette purchase. But maybe that's it! What were some of the key lines from my dream?

Do I truly yearn?

Can't decide with a blissful heart

No trumpets heard.

I've just poured my morning coffee, while sitting at the table waiting for the toast to pop up. I'm beginning to get the picture. Despite Kelly's approval and a chance to snag a once in a lifetime opportunity, this Vette purchase goes against every standard or every value, where I have put my faith and found happiness. True, I was experiencing uncertainly in reaching a decision. This is precisely why I took it to the Lord in prayer. I've realized I was looking for change for all the wrong reasons. I was amiss in my thinking, in turn in my asking. I was moving on to a new chapter in my life, and a different type of car from my traditional norm, sounded like a great way to celebrate the occasion. In reality, deep down I knew I was never comfortable with the idea of buying a Vette. I was trying to convince myself this was what I wanted. At the same time, I was looking to the Good Lord to bless the whole thing, rendering it a done deal. Yes, I got His response; it was revealing and forthright as I heard it. His reply was as jumbled as my idea to purchase a Vette in the first place. To be honest, many of my recent thoughts on buying the Vette were actually quite similar to those I received in the poem. I was hoping I would convince myself otherwise.

The sleek and stylish Corvette is simply not for me. This is not at all meant to disparage this classic vehicle. The Corvette is a super sweet ride and a pillar of success in the automotive industry. Many people are well suited to be seated behind the wheel of this fine automobile, I'm just not one of them.

Jesus will guide us, whether our questions are simple or difficult. In all His wisdom and perfection, He will safely navigate us down the proper path. As well, He will let us know when we simply are barking up the wrong tree, or when we are trying to fit a square peg into a round hole. In other words, we will be reminded when we are only using our head as a hat rack.

During my dream, I swung on the familiar bench, with golden yellow and red leaves abound. These leaves lived out their time on the trees above, and then fluttered to the ground when the time was right. Fallen, along with these leaves are my thoughts on buying a Vette; the car which I had only casually considered as a true must have. As the leaves decay into the ground to regenerate the Earth, my thinking needs a similar revival. I am able to do that through the direction of our Lord: by praying, and by listening to my heart.

He is so good to us. How can you not love Him to pieces?

Age 43

They Pay Me to do This

1990

Eight years have passed by since we moved here from Ohio. Our family faithfully stepped in the trust of the Lord's assuring words, and made the move to South Carolina. That same conviction remains as strong in our hearts today as it did then. Make no mistake; we absolutely cherished life in Ohio. We left family, friends, and countless memories behind. In exchange, we were welcomed by the warm people of the Carolinas, and gifted the endless beauty of this area. To keep us close with our northern contingent, our dear Lord guided us to reunite with old friends from Ohio, to again enjoy their loving hearts and always remember their kind friendship.

I dearly love the Carolinas, and I truly love what I do for a living. When I was in Ohio, I enjoyed being in the Industrial tool business. I adored our home and my time in the yard; planting, gardening, and tending to the Earth's generous yield. Kelly and I are passionate about nature. We'd work endless hours elbow to elbow with the spirit of Jesus in the welcoming sunshine. We'd coddle and encourage our tender growth, and share with anyone who wanted to sample the fruits of our harvest. Today, working in the tool supply side of the nursery allows me to enjoy both aspects of the business. I remain fascinated and well versed in the beauty and complexity of our tool and machine line. Yet I never miss a day wandering the grounds of the nursery. Usually around noon, I stroll through the yard and take in the sights and smells of the amazing products we feature. From flowers to plants, sand and mulch, from pavers to rock and boulders, to logs and timbers, we stock everything one would need to create a memorable back yard oasis. The kind of yard one would never want to leave; the stuff "staycations" are made of exists in our blessed three and a half acres of paradise. I honestly think our staff could design a yard of such alluring beauty; the ambience would suggest an Eden like ambience. I'm sure God has prepared our eternal home with indescribable detail, but our Heaven on Earth is a blessing I will gladly accept for now. Picture this; a stylish water feature babbling through your property, alongside paved walkways meandering through a tasteful arrangement of colorful flowers and unique plants. All of which leads to a beautiful vegetable garden flourishing in unmatched varieties of succulent and delicious fruits and vegies. This is the potential of our wonderful product, and best of all... I get paid to be part of this. Nothing could be better, thank you Jesus!

At the end of each day, as I leave the nursery, I take a right turn on the highway and head home. I get the pleasure of passing by the place where I just spent my day. The industrial building is still new and is surrounded by some seriously impressive graders and excavators. I pass by the Nursery yard which houses mounds of dirt, sand, rock and mulch; the dream stuff of any landscaper. All of which are all sectioned off in their own personal dens, at the ready to fill our customer's imaginings with the landscaping desires of their wishes. Three and a half precious acres of the coolest stuff in the world and I'm blessed to be among this glorious haven of yard bling from Monday through Friday.

Tonight, after dinner I chatted with Kelly about work. Our kids, both in High school, were out for the evening. Dana was with friends and Brandon was attending a school concert. As an educator, Kelly has been teaching third grade for the past five years, and in total teaching for the past twenty years. We often talk about how grateful we are to be working in fields that we truly enjoy. I jokingly insist I love my job more. Not that it's a contest, but when It comes to loving what you do for a living, no matter who I liken my career to, I feel I'll win that comparison. "Good for you dear", Kelly would say in an encouraging burst. "You keep working hard, love what you do, be hugely successful, make lots of money and I'll retire!" Leave it to my encouraging and fast thinking wife, to always know just what to say.

We decided to turn in a bit early. It was Thursday evening and Friday promised to be a long day. After work we will be heading to the lake for the weekend. We are going to be scoping out some waterfront acreage. We are considering a nice tract which can accommodate lake shore camping, water sports and possibly be suitable to build a cottage for weekend getaways. I have had thoughts of building a home for retirement on such a location, but we really don't know where we want to be when fulltime retirement is upon us. No rush; we're only in our early forties; there is ample time for those plans to play out.

The thought of enjoying a pleasant and relaxing leave the wristwatch at home type weekend with Kelly, and whoever Jesus puts in our path will be a blessing. We'll check out some land options, eat when we are hungry, and call it a day when we're ready to retire for the evening. It'll be just us and Jesus chilling together.

I think Jesus is right there with us in thought, as we get ready to enjoy our time with Him. Take a listen to what He shared with me during the overnight...

Awaken My son
Well you have rested
To enjoy your life work
Where your heart is invested
Where grief shall not lurk
And your soul is not tested

If joy is at work
You'll ne'er toil a day
No scowls or worry
Joy reigns over pay
The clock need not hurry
To tick moments away

Treat every person
As though family or friend
If anxieties rise
Relief I will send
Each day I will guard you
From morn to days end

Put other hearts first
Your account shall grow
All ills will disperse
Your elation will flow
May life be enriched
By the seeds which you sew

This is a lovely way to start out the day. Jesus and I have got this. If I start to fade, He will replenish; if I wilt, He will water; should I fall; He will cradle. My willingness to support and help others will be my joy as much as theirs.

It's a good thing He reminded me of His readiness to support all of our earnest efforts. This day has proven to be a trying one. Two of our vender trucks, which arrive at dawn, were late due to an early morning tie-up on the freeway. This put our truck, which normally departs for our deliveries at 8:00 AM, over an hour late. The nursery opens at the crack of dawn, so our customers receive their goods, supplies and landscaping needs early, allowing them to get in a full day's work. We pray these delays be few and far between, but it is the nature of the business. We also pray for those involved in the incident, those tending to them, and for the safety of our drivers, as they hurry to get our product delivered once they get on the road.

Unfortunately, as the day progressed, (perhaps regressed would be more appropriate) the fun didn't stop there. We learned there will be a recall on one of our popular weed trimmers. It seems the fuel cap can possibly work loose from vibration, during extended periods of use. It is a precautionary recall, and a time-consuming process. One final bit of excitement, a front loader accidently backed into a concrete dividing wall, toppling it to the ground. This particular barrier separated a section of dirt and sand from another. We now have a hybrid mix of black top soil and concrete mix sand. Looks like a giant oversized marble cake mix adorning our yard. An unfortunate mess, but we will deal with it; Lord give us strength.

Able to avert additional disasters, it was time to close up shop. This was a day which tested our patience and challenged our bottom line. It was one of those days which confirms we are guaranteed times of trial and tribulation. Fortunately for all concerned during these delays and problems, no one was hurt, and everyone was able to safely return home at day ends. This was a true blessing when considering some of the possible outcomes. We could have chosen to be flustered over the waste and cost of today's events. Instead our crew was thankful the Lord had us in His arms the entire time, possibly easing some of the damage and protecting those of us who could have been injured. For me it is faith and trust and thank You Jesus, for another day shared with You. It's all good.

As evening came, I shared the calamity of events which we endured at the nursery. It seems like I wasn't alone in the "guess what happened at work today" category. Kelly told us of a glitch in the bell system at school. They had a fire drill scheduled, and for some reason after the four-short burst of bells sounded, the last ring never stopped. The deafening sound went on for a solid forty-five minutes. Finally, someone from the alarm service disabled the bell system so it could be repaired. This meant the entire school had to remain outside the building on the playground. Due to safety regulations no students can be in the school building, if the alarm system is down. Today, our beautiful Carolina fall day featured a lovely 91 degrees. The kids were hot and getting a bit antsy, as they simmered on the playground. Fortunately, just about the time the principal had to make a decision on what to do about the situation, it was announced the bell system was again fully operational, and the kids could reenter the building.

Sometime during the time, the repairs were being made, as workmen went in and out of the building, a large sheep dog must have gotten out of his yard and decided to attend school. He took advantage of the open doors and entered the school escaping the ninety plus degree weather. He followed his nose into the cafeteria and was lured out of the kitchen area, by a quick-thinking custodian who enticed the uninvited guest through the halls with a plate full of meat loaf. The sheep dog was slightly distracted by the cheering students on their way back to the class rooms, but he intently followed Mr. Phillips as he swiftly made his way through the hall, in pursuit of the *mystery meat*. Animal control was waiting outside, and after our shaggy trespasser enjoyed his lunch, they took it from there. At least he was taken into custody on a full tummy, as he waited to be reunited with his owner.

As Kelly and I discussed our events of the day, we managed to find humor is some these misfortunes, though they were hardly laughing matters at the time. For the most part these happenings we more inconveniences than long term problems. Still, some were issues that have to be worked out, but we at the nursery, as well as those on the school staff, know we've got this. We and Jesus can work out anything that life sets before us. Everyone will return to work and school tomorrow and a new day will be upon us.

As evening came to an end and bedtime arrived, Kelly and I again prayed in thanks to Jesus for navigating us through our *interesting* days. I started to dream and found myself on one of the swinging benches we sell at the nursery. I quietly gazed at our vast and varied inventory. Just about the time I was to glance over at our new top soil and sand blend, my attention was diverted to these reassuring words...

I am here
From now without end
Every turn each moment
I'll comfort I'll mend

Trust no ill wind
Shall enter or gain
An upper hand
On those I sustain

Stride in faith
On my trusting path
When in My fold
My light will be cast

There will always be trials
To navigate through
Let us step wisely
Faithfully true

As storms try to rattle
And shake our day
Keep pace in my sureness
I am the way

I soon awoke to a peaceful Friday morning. The sun had just begun peering through the dogwoods in our back yard. A few rays slipped through the barely opened vertical blinds and managed to reach us still lying in bed. It was early fall and the promise of a splendid autumn day was calling. Kelly opened her eyes, squinting away the uninvited rays, while sporting a satisfying smile. The thought of Friday is always a welcome notion and assists us when getting up. In Kelly's case, her larger than normal grin could be due to her having an "in service day". This means school for her, but no students, and likely a quieter day than yesterday.

As for me, I have a nice full Friday on tap. What a joy it is to be working at a place which sells the tools and products, the likes of which can create an Eden like landscape of boundless possibility. I'm likely stretching it a bit suggesting we are able to craft lush and dreamlike gardens of heavenly proportions. But until the day we actually enter those breath-taking gardens, we here at Carolina Garden and Equipment want to make every effort for the customer to come as close as they can. After all, when you enjoy what you do, it's not work, it's a pleasure!

Age 44

The Sun Rises on My Son

1991

When I look at my son Brandon, I see much of myself in him. We just celebrated his sixteenth birthday. As an eleventh grader he has excelled greatly in many areas, and less in others. Whereas I had my strong suits in speech and language, Brandon shines in mathematics and the sciences. Numbers, formulas, equations and all things math describe him. He is fiscally wise and one could say he is just short of being considered a human calculator. He's the kind of kid that would choose advanced economics as an elective. From his earliest days he had a tendency to save wisely. He sold or traded things and organized his baseball card collection, like an accounting firm prepping for an audit.

I'm not suggesting my son is strictly a numbers driven, value minded scrooge; Brandon is a humorous, loving, warm and generous young man. He possesses a clever wit and is very giving of his time. This semester he is tutoring two days a week after school. One day he tutors a boy on math and the other day a student in chemistry. He does this unselfishly and I could not be prouder of him.

One day after school, a few months back, Brandon shared some news about a district sponsored writing contest. Being the word geek that I still am, my eyes brightened and my ears perked up like a kid hearing the bells chiming from an ice cream truck. More so I was elated that he had an interest in entering. "So, what is the contest about", I questioned. "Basically", he started," we are to write about a skill or interest we have and how we apply that ability in a positive manner. Perhaps we use it to help others or our community, or even ourselves. The contest is titled *A World Prepared through Skills Shared"*, he concluded. Now this is the kind of contest I would be all over. For a brief moment I was immersed in thought as to what direction I would take in the contest. That fleeting thought quickly vanished once I realized the excitement Brandon was experiencing about entering the contest. He is a math and science guy; absorbed in numbers, equations, formulas and conclusions based on facts. Writing words on paper is far more freeform allowing the writer to take inner thoughts in limitless directions. By no means am I classifying my son as a cut and dried math equation, but I am pleasantly surprised he has an interest to diverse his skill set in a creative and thought-provoking way...

voluntarily no less. It is a bit out of his wheel house, but I for one am excited to see this side of him and view his finished product.

"Any ideas as to what are you going to write about", I questioned? "Actually, I know exactly what I'm going to write about", Brandon quickly and confidently responded. "I love math and numbers and the precision of the subject; I have a passion for science and the formulas and facts which define its nature; but many people are overwhelmed by these subjects. They often are intimidated by the precision of the subject and feel it's too difficult to understand, never mind master. While tutoring, I work on any small victory my students accomplish and build their confidence through the success of understanding one equation or problem at a time. Soon they realize what doesn't come naturally can still be learned and even mastered." Wow, very nice approach son. That is taking a skill and applying it to others if I ever heard it! I am proud of Brandon on so many levels. I am pleased he is using his talent in a voluntary manner to enter the contest; but I am far more delighted that his tutoring skills are going further than simply teaching a student a subject. He is encouraging and mentoring them on important life qualities, such as confidence and determination.

Later that evening as we readied for bed, Kelly and I continued our conversation about Brandon. We both agreed, regardless of the outcome of the contest, his intend and approach to mentoring and tutoring students, is far more satisfying and important than any contest results.

As I journaled my love and appreciation for my son, I closed the day with a joy filled heart. I learned much about his dedication toward others and how he truly strives to make a positive difference in other's lives. Overnight, while in blissful sleep, Jesus added this footnote...

Far beyond a want to win
A passion drives his desire
Worthy is his calling higher
To help his fellow kin

Let no equation define the will
That ushers him to wisely teach
Those in need so they will reach
The knowledge to hone their skills

Compassion fills our eager son
To share his caring mind
To fashion words, succinct and kind
So answers come to everyone

The sun shall rise on your youthful kin
And those who seek and yearn
To absorb so they will learn
How far they came from where they'd been

His life so blessed... your son will win

What a great sleep I received. What a fantastic message I received from Jesus. The Lord spoke fondly of Brandon; His message was revealing and was filled with pleasantries and positives. Jesus clearly shared the qualities of Brandon's generous nature and his willingness to help others improve not only in subject matter but in self-assurance. In confidence there is victory; this is a skill that these or any students will benefit from over and over during their lifetimes. If we allow our skills and desires to be known, Jesus will offer His direction. Who better knows us than Jesus? He knows our every thought, both courageous and worrisome; He knows our feelings, whatever they may be, and He keeps us whole in the process, if we allow Him to do so. The passion which Brandon expressed yesterday blessed both Kelly and me. The last line of the poem I will share with Kelly, but I will discreetly keep those words from Brandon. He is aware of my poetic communications, but he doesn't much ask about them. I think he simply leaves them for me to receive and enjoy. Will he win the contest? I have it on good advice he may or at least will win something. We shall see.

As we entered the first of April, the school year was closing in on the last two months of the spring semester. Brandon and his students continue to meet and study in preparation for upcoming finals. Between school, his club activities, and a part-time job at the hardware store, Brandon continued to work on his paper for the contest. With the deadline fast approaching, he finished his submission. He seemed pleased with the results, but voiced no concern of the outcome. As he put it, he is happy with the paper, but happier his tutors were gaining an understanding of the text and making progress every day. Given the modest, ego free personality of my son, I honestly believe him when he says the paper is just that, simply something to submit and share. I think it also lets him better process what he actually does, so he can critique his methods, should he tutor as a senior. I guess his biggest concern is... actually... I don't what concerns he has; school wise anyway. At sixteen he seems to have it far more together than I did at his age. I was a self-conscious social mess. He seems well rounded, dates and has lots of friends, gets good grades, and certainly is generous and unselfish with his time and skills. It is clear he receives great satisfaction when helping others. Much like his compassionate mother did, when she selflessly gave herself at the children's cancer ward back in Ohio. The Lord has blessed my son with many redeeming characteristics; that awareness is paramount when attempting to live life to the fullest. That is Kelly's key to embracing the joys of life and Brandon seems to have harnessed that wonderful Webster quality.

Early May has arrived and we have enjoyed blooms and blossoms for several weeks. The trees and shrubs are fully green, and with summer just around the corner the school year is coming to a close. Kelly and her third graders are enjoying a year end field trip to the petting farm, somewhere over the border in North Carolina. Dana will soon be coming home from her first year at college. At work we are in the heart of our planting, growing and building season. It seems we are all in the midst of preparing for summer and our hot Carolina summer months.

As our son Brandon wraps up his tutoring duties, the results of the writing contest were announced today. Our modest son was needless to say elated with the outcome. For his worthy efforts he received one of three honorable mentions. This is an achievement any young writer and supporting parents should be very proud of. Congratulations young man; well done.

Two weeks later, with the last of the school days on countdown to summer vacation, Brandon came home sporting an ear to ear smile. His look of elation could easily rival any morning smile Jesus and I ever displayed. It was close to 6:00 pm, and earlier he had called home saying he'd be a little late, but will be home for dinner. Results from finals had just come in and he and his two tutor students we celebrating at a fast food place. Brandon was pleased to find out his Algebra student scored an 89 and his chemistry student a 91. Both kids were beyond words of thanks for our caring son.

That evening after dinner, Dana (already home from college) just returned from the bakery with a congratulation cake for her brother. Dana was unaware of Brandon's contest entry and his heroic efforts in successfully tutoring over this past year. Once she learned of his unselfish work to help those in need and his desire to write about his passion, she couldn't have been prouder of her younger sibling.

After dinner before enjoying Dana's tasty treat, she asked if she could say grace before sharing cake and family discussion. Here are her words….

Father we give much thanks for all the wonderful things you give us every day. As we prepare to share this cake in celebration, I want to also give thanks for the loving guidance you have given Brandon this past year. His caring heart has helped two students achieve the understand they were lacking to attain a successful school year. You also guided my brother in mind and spirit, so he could put into words a paper which captured the joy of this experience. He did not win the contest, but he is a winner in their hearts and ours for his great efforts and achievements. I could not be prouder of him. Thank you for Your ever-trusting guidance and presence as we celebrate with this cake. In your blessed name, Amen.

Immediately after Dana's amen, Kelly rose and went over to Dana to give her a motherly hug, she continued around the table giving me a wink and a peck on the cheek, then arrived to Brandon who had already stood up to receive her hugs. This was a perfect family moment; one which will remain in memory forever. I don't think I ever enjoyed cake any more than this one. We ate and chatted for an hour as Dana asked question after question about his tutoring and his desire to put it into words.

As Dana and Brandon carried much of the conversation, Kelly and I exchanged smiles, winks and feelings of happiness, as the banter between these two loving siblings continued. I thought back to Dana's prayer about her brother. Her referring to him as a winner in the hearts of his two tutors clearly resonates in the words of Jesus from my poem last month. The sun indeed does shine brightly on our son Brandon, and on those who learn from his caring heart. Brandon's faith and trust in Jesus gets stronger every day. He has recognized the importance of his skills and the potential to make a difference in all of our lives. He indeed is a winner! Amen!

Age 45

Dana Designs Her Destiny

1992

Our daughter Dana Louise is a lovely example of the impeccable workmanship of God. She is a clone of her mother in every aspect of her beautiful make up, both inside and out. In addition, she was blessed with artistic and imaginative genes. These God given blessings drive and encourage her to design, build and create. Dana exhibited these skills early and often in her young life. Her bedroom, for example, was repainted, repurposed, reinvented and re-everything'd more times than I can recall. She, more so than her brother, was the child who wanted to design and build a tree fort, though the fort was intended for Brandon and his pals. I don't recall if she ever went up into the fort, but she did experience great pleasure in assisting in the build and seeing it to completion.

Shortly after that project was completed, she along with Daryl and me built a playhouse. The structure was designed on the fly and actually became a two-room house, 12 x 16 feet with a small loft, serving as a sleeping area.   Dana became, albeit self-appointed, the cite coordinator of the project. To complete her look, and observing safety first, she donned her Cleveland Indians souvenir batting helmet, in hard hat tradition. Amazingly at nine she did most of the decorating and with some direction from Kelly, made drapes for all the windows in her little bungalow. She furnished her cozy little abode, courtesy of Good Will purchases and scouring yard sales for choice pieces. Her garage sale prowess came under the guidance and tutelage of Kelly; the apple doesn't fall too far from the tree.

Given the background of Dana's creative design and building skills, it came as no surprise she would seek further education in the building and design industry. Kelly and I had started college funds for both children, but as often is the case the funds left a bit to be desired. In her senior year of high school, after contributing a couple of successful designing efforts for two school plays, she was able to co-op at a building supply house. This gave her excellent exposure in the building trades. The supply house was owned and managed by a college alumnus from the university Dana is eying. He very quickly noticed Dana's skills, tenacity and diligent work ethic. His name is Tim Brenner and he was kind enough to provide a letter of recommendation on her behalf, to the school.   Along with that endorsement and others, as well as endless efforts on Dana's part to apply for scholarship money anywhere she could; she received a partial scholarship at the school's department of architecture. , I am as proud as can be by what Dana has accomplished in her young life. Believe me, we will celebrate this wonderful occasion, *but* it is important to be thankful and understand all success is through grace and grace alone.

I have always viewed any accomplishment as achieved through the will and desire of God. While we as individuals fulfill the work and deeds of that will, it is not without the strength and guidance of Jesus. I think it important to stay grounded in the celebration of those successes in what I call "guarded excitement". Make no mistake I believe Dana is fully appreciative of her wonderful opportunity. She has confidence in her ability, and fully intends to be successful. I get the feeling she will embrace every moments, none of which will be too big for her to handle. In time, her successes in life will best define her in two words; confident and independent. But right now, and forever, I'll still go with sweet and beautiful. After all, despite her maturity, poise and preparedness, she always will be daddy's little girl.

As the summer pushed on and August entered the scene, Dana is in final prep to get ready to move into her dorm. However, in just the past couple of days, I have been undergoing some anxiety as I realize the magnitude of this major change in our lives. I am totally confident she is ready for this major step in her life, and will embrace it to the fullest. I simply need to let go of her, and figure out how I am going to refill the hole that remains.

Later in the afternoon, we made plans to meet Dana for dinner at Smokey's Grill for some fabulous Carolina barbeque. We enjoyed some masterfully prepared tender beef medallions, basked in Smokey's magical sauce. Dana was excited and was bursting with new information about the school and her curriculum. She and Kelly carried on most of the conversation, as I smiled and simply enjoyed the moment and Dana's enthusiasm. Yet, in the back of my mind I was still resisting a bit to relinquish my little girl to the demands and the responsibility of higher education. This was a day I knew would eventually come, so it was the time to suck it up and enjoy the evening with my girls.

On the way home we decided to stop at the outlet mall. The girls wanted to do some impromptu shopping and pick up a few extra items for the dorm. I chose to browse the sporting goods stores and also check out the tool outlet. It's a great mind relaxer to ogle over all the tools I wish I had, but in all likelihood, would rarely use. The evening was pleasant so after browsing, I found a comfortable bench outside the Kitchen Deluxe. I waited for the girls to exit the store, as I gave my blessings for a beautiful and enjoyable evening. Once they came out, we called it a day and headed back to our house.

Upon arriving home, we had little energy left in the tank. The bags of spoils remained in their respective packages, and the left-over Smokey's went into the fridge. There is nothing better than left over barbeque and a cold glass of milk for breakfast the next day. Just fry an egg or two and slide it over the reheated barbeque. In my opinion if eggs are involved, that constitutes a legitimate breakfast. Try it some time.

Just before we tucked in for the night Dana came into our room, announcing she had two things to say. First, thanks for dinner and shopping, second and more importantly, that she loved both of us very much. I wonder if the separation is also weighing a bit on her mind. I say that because her voice cracked slightly as she said she loved us. She is such a beauty inside and out. Love ya back sweetie!

After Dana's good night visit, it was lights out and prayers and blessings to Jesus for the wonderful day. Perhaps there was a sense of apprehension in my prayers tonight, but as He often does, Jesus offered His calming touch to soften my worries...

Each child is special, no two the same
In His creation, just as they came
Love and accept them, no cause for alarm
I'll help you defend and protect them from harm

One moment she'll teeter
From Mom's arms to Dad
No time is sweeter
All hearts are glad

As a river she'll flow
And then become stronger
Her being will grow
She's a child no longer

She grew as you mentored
She's smart and she's skilled
Her life is well centered
Through what We've instilled

As morning broke, after sharing my daily greeting with Jesus, I began formulating my thoughts from last night's guidance. A number of things were felt in that dream with regard to separation. College is a memorable time for everyone in the family. Whether it is Mom or Dad, a younger sibling, or the off spring beginning a new chapter in their life, emotions can go from hope, optimism, and eagerness to anxiety, nervousness and trepidation, in an instant. The umbilical cord can only stretch so far, and then it has to be cut.

The words I received last night were a reminder of what I already had learned from Jesus. We have guided our children well and always allowed them the freedom of choosing wisely for themselves. Kelly and I have centered our lives on trust and respect, and have never exhibited anything other than esteem and admiration toward one other, whether the children were present or not. We simply did this out of love and respect for each other. I think the children grew up and naturally learned the importance of accountability and respect, through the relationship Kelly and I demonstrated. Jesus took our hand as we adjusted to life together as a couple. He also took the hands of our children; and taught them to take these values with them, where ever their daily journey leads.

My father was not a man of great or memorable oral passages, but I do recall, on more than one occasion, him saying *there is no substitute for good manners*. Good manners set the foundation for decency, respect, and simple common curtesy. These important qualities, under the guidance of Jesus, invite positive experiences to enter our lives.

As the Good Lord guided Mom and Dad, when raising Daryl and me, He did the same for me and Kelly, as we mentored our children. I think I can worry and fret about Dana all I want, as she enters this new chapter in her life. The Lord will let me do that if I choose; He is all about freedom and will allow me to struggle if I insist. Eventually, my frustrations will become too much. I'll accept she is no longer my little girl, but a young woman about to take her place in the world. I'll then realize

Jesus will be where He was all along; waiting for me with open arms, assuring me He will guide Dana every step of the way.

 After absorbing last night's assurance and guidance, I think I'm ready to let he go and conquer the world. I know she can do it!

Age 46

Daryl and Sherry

1993

I have spoken endlessly about the blessings Kelly and I continually receive from our loving families. Our parents immediately come to mind when speaking about our two clans. I have not however, shared nearly enough about the heart of my caring big brother Daryl. He and his wife Sherry are among the most unselfish and giving people I have been blessed to know.

Experiencing true brotherly love is one of life's great gifts. There are certain particulars which seem to accompany this special relationship. Still, as boys three years apart, maturity levels between us often fell out of balance and tested our relationship. Let's just say our bond occasionally became rockier than loving. I frequently found myself on the receiving end of a loving pounding. No bruises were inflicted since Daryl gamely held back. It was all good, particularly when big brother let little bro get in a couple of courtesy shots. Fortunately for me, Daryl possessed a natural tendency to adhere to the rules of fair play. He knew deep down my only desire was to fellowship with him and his friends. I knew I had to display my A game if I wanted to be included in any of his social activities.

I specifically recall when Daryl was sixteen; his girlfriend visited the house one Saturday afternoon. Prior to leaving to take in a blood curdling black and white double feature at the Midtown, he and Julie called me into the kitchen to share a Coke and some small talk. To be included in their personal time was very special to me. I make these points to let you know Daryl is a great guy and an exceptional brother. At forty-nine he remains a selfless and kind man possessing a generous Christian heart. Daryl, you are the best!

Fast forward to present day, my brother and his wonderful wife Sherry continue demonstrating the traits of thoughtful and caring people. Unfortunately, they have never been blessed with a family of their own. They and Jesus have learned to live with the fact that they likely will never be able to have children. Despite that reality, my brother Daryl is an absolute gem of an uncle to my kids. In fact he is kind to everyone who is fortunate enough to make his acquaintance.

Recently Daryl and Sherry have upped their game and last year they qualified themselves to become foster parents. There are tens of thousands of foster kids in need of loving homes. So, my brother, at the age of forty-nine and Sherry at forty-five, made the gracious decision to foster a brother and sister. These two precious children are Laura, seven and Freddy, nine. They lost their parents in a house fire six years ago. They spent the last four years in the foster system. While the Good Lord kept them together, they are still looking for their forever home. Daryl and Sherry then came into their lives. After several visits and all the appropriate measures met, my big bro and his wife became proud foster parents to the Weller kids. About a year has passed and their beautiful family is about to celebrate Laura's eighth birthday.

As a little brother myself, I have had the advantage of learning from an older sibling. Sometimes learning from his mistakes, but far more often learning by the examples he successfully demonstrated. He and Sherry have a beautiful home near Mom and Dad's place. Daryl has successfully partnered with Dad at their shop, since he came on board back in eighty-one. More important than business success and a nice house, Daryl and Sherry have decided to take things a step further. I just learned from Kelly, via a two-hour phone all with Sherry, they are seriously considering adopting these two great kids, as their own.

Typically foster kids stay with their host family for about two years. Their first two foster families were examples of that average. But something special has happened for them this time around. Daryl and Freddy both love the outdoors. They are in heaven when hiking, fishing, camping or anything involving being out in the fresh air, including going to Toledo Mud Hen games. For a while now Daryl has been bringing Freddy to the shop on weekends, when there is catch up work to be done. Freddy is learning to clean and sort parts, and enjoys the hands-on aspect of learning the business. My dad is ecstatic with the thought of the next generation already even slightly involved in the business. Laura and Sherry are inseparable. Sherry is a lawyer at her father's firm, and has taken a leave from the practice, since they began fostering. One of the partners at their firm has been working with a practice that specializes on adoption proceedings. Daryl and Sherry are excited to share their home with Laura and Freddy and someday their home could become a permanent residence for the Weller kids.

Since we've moved to South Carolina, we have made every effort to visit family back in Toledo as often as possible. However this year Daryl, Sherry and the kids are going to visit us in South Carolina. Dana and Brandon are older than Daryl's two, but are willing to take the time to meet their new cousins and take them to some exciting places, while forming their new family bond. Now that its summer time, Daryl can finally get away from the shop, (he's like Dad in that regard) and we have a lot of catching up to do, and questions for them on their adoption decision.

Yesterday afternoon Daryl and company arrived at our home. After a warm greeting over some of Kelly's Carolina barbeque, and an evening chat, Daryl's group was ready to get a good night's sleep before officially starting their vacation in the morning. It was decided our kids would take Daryl and Sherry's two to the amusement park. Dana is home on summer break after her third year of college, and Brandon just graduated high school and is working part time at the nursery. This will give Kelly and me an entire day to catch up with D&S and discuss their life changing decision to adopt the Weller kids. I have seen the kids on one other occasion, and I don't think the good Lord has ever made two more appreciative kids. Living in foster care can be difficult and trying, particularly when the kids are as young as these two. Think about it, this is the forth family theses young siblings have lived with. I'm sure the kid's hopes and spirits are high, and as much as they love Daryl and Sherry, disappointment often accompanies child placement when it comes to the foster system. I may be a bit bias but their desire to have D&S as adoptive parents would be a great fit for them. I'm sure Jesus will extend his guiding hand toward all concerned and encourage this adoption to go through, when the time is right.

Now late in the afternoon, Dana and Brandon just returned home with the kids. Rides and lots of water park activities have produced a couple of tired but happy young kids.   Sherry's sunscreen rule was dutifully followed by Dana so the kids came home no worse for the wear. It is time for a nice balanced home cooked meal, to counter the dogs and sodas which no doubt was consumed at the park.

By mid-evening Laura was snoozing on the sofa, and Freddy was fighting the heavy eyelids with the best of them. We chatted till 9:15 PM, and then Sherry tucked the kids in for the night. I was again super impressed with the manners of their two kids. I was just as proud of my own children. Clearly Dana is filling the big sister role that Laura has always wanted. I was also pleased how much face time Brandon gave to Freddy, in sharing his Nintendo skills over much of the evening. Super big hugs were given to our kids by D&S, for their willingness to show these two sweet children a good time and extend some family cousin lovin'.

After the girls stepped into the kitchen to put away the rest of the evening snacks, I took Daryl into the family room for a quick game of darts. This was the first time he and I had a chance to chat one on one since they had arrived. "So Daryl, I started. "I've got to say your two kids are fantastic. What are your thoughts on them; on the future"?   We hit the pause button on our dart throwing, and faced each other as Daryl began to speak... "You know Dan, years ago Sherry and I learned having children is not going to happen. For reasons only known to God, this is our reality. It's a situation we struggled with but have accepted. Our conclusion is God knows our hearts and He has a plan for us. Mostly due to Sherry's perspective, she insisted we not rush into things. Live each day as it comes and enjoy the fruits of that day" ... (this sounds like *let no joy go unclaimed* at its very best). "Anyway", Daryl continued, "We believe good things come to those that wait. As much as we love these kids, we wanted to make sure this is a perfect fit for all four of us. We're still new at fostering and connecting on the right children the first time around seemed too good to be true. Let's give credit to the system and give them their due that they matched us well with these two great kids. We've taken our decision to Jesus in prayer for several weeks, and we are not getting back any worrisome thoughts. I truly think the Lord is urging us to adopt. Perhaps we will get final confirmation in our hearts this week while visiting. If so, that would be a wonderful addition to our vacation", Daryl said in closing. I think Daryl and Sherry have an excellent handle on things and I believe Jesus will let him know if that is indeed the case.

As we turned in for the night, Kelly and I said an extra prayer for D&S over their pending decision. Kelly loves the two little Weller kids and told Sherry, even though we are two states away, we will support their decision and offer our hearts, our home and our time to them always.

As I close my eyes, I take my thoughts of Daryl and the family in prayer to Jesus, and loving ask He guide and direct them. I asked He ease their hearts and hold them close. Overnight, these words were shared with me...

You did not rush
Or step ahead
Of my guidance
As you are led

Keep Me in focus
Choose well and right
I'll cast no shadow
To distort your sight

Let doubt be bid
A fond farewell
Be free forever
Of its spell

Let minds be certain
Rest in this word
Your children's wishes
Will now be heard

Immediately after I received this timely passage, I awoke. I was surprised to see the clock read 1:35 AM. This dream came early in the overnight and now I'm wide awake. I wish I could wake Daryl and tell him about my dream. But it would be a bit much to wake him and lay this on him in the wee hours of the morning. Time to take the advice of the first stanza in the poem … don't rush, or step ahead. I'll take a deep breath and let the comfort of His word lead me back to sleep.

The next morning, I curiously asked Daryl how he slept. "I slept great", Daryl replied. "Where ever we go or whatever we do, I will be spending my day with the people that mean the most to me; my brother and his kind family and my special family". Sherry smiled lifting her juice glass in toast of Daryl comments. Daryl lifted his glass as well then turned to his kids. "Also", Daryl continued," to my loving kids, the children who I want to spend the rest of my life with"! Daryl must have heard from Jesus as well! The table burst forth in cheer. Daryl's kids bolted from their chairs, and raced to hug their daddy to be. Sherry began tearing up and Kelly and I were not far behind.

What a glorious morning. Indeed it will be a wonderful day as Daryl stated. As Jesus spoke to me about His plans for Daryl and family, He clearly eased Daryl's mind and encouraged him to trust his heart. I think Jesus also assured Daryl, he and Sherry are the best He has to give the Wellers their forever home. What a blessing the kids and D&S are to each other. What a blessing for me that Jesus shared His wisdom, which He imparted onto my brother!

Age 48

To Move or not to Move

1995

We have lived in the beautiful Southeast, since our move from Ohio in 1981. From my observations the Carolinas basically have two seasons; ten months of summer and two months of jacket weather. Call those two months either fall or spring, but we simply do not have a true winter season. Do we have cold days? Yes. Do we get some snow? Again yes, but not every year. You'd better take a picture if you want to remember what it looked like... it won't last long.

I must admit I did enjoy the beauty of winter's freshly fallen snow, as it gently glistened in the early Ohio Winter mornings. A peaceful memory of simpler times as a child comes to mind. But I do not miss the fact that large amounts or even untimely amounts of snow could dictate our vulnerable winter lives. Snow shovels, snow plows and ice melt notwithstanding, falling prey to winter weather is common place in northern Ohio, despite being equipped to battle this cold weather intruder. By comparison, a good snow here in upstate South Carolina is more like a token dusting, in our former home state. I bring weather into the conversation, since a possible move is looming large for the Lowe family. Unfortunately, we would be exchanging the beauty of the Carolinas, for the extreme conditions experienced north of here.

I have been given the prospect to relocate back to the western suburbs of Cleveland, Ohio. It is a move which would include the joys of Lake Erie blanketing multiple inches of lake effect snow over the greater Cleveland area. That undesirable bullet point would appear on the negative side of the ledger, when listing the pluses and minuses of our major upcoming decision. The consideration to move has come into play, as a result of an opportunity, extended to me by my former employer. Two carrots hang dangling on a string in front of me. The ever-tempting major increase in pay and a giant step up the corporate ladder are the key selling points. Specifically, I have been offered the prospect to manage the entire east coast division. I never lost total contact with my old company. Due to the retirement of the current manager and another upper management figure leaving, I got a call to see if I was interested in reupping.

To be sure, this is quite an honor, but I am at a real crossroads here! First, Kelly and I and the kids love the Carolinas. I mean really; what's not to love? We have great weather, wonderful people and we're just hours from either the mountains or the ocean. It's perfect. On the other hand, Brandon is twenty and in college. He is commuting from home to save money, but would have no problem finding living quarters on his own. Dana, now twenty-two, has graduated and is in commercial decorating and design. She has an apartment and is more reliable and independent as a self-winding Swiss time-piece. With that said I cannot use the off spring as a reason for refusal. Kelly is a teacher and can likely secure work in any of the school districts in the surrounding Cleveland area. As well Kelly's favorite Aunt Carla and Uncle Bob and cousins are in the greater Cleveland area. I suspect Kelly would support the move if I insisted. With all this said, the decision looms largely if not entirely on my desire to relocate, cash in on a salary windfall, and move up a rung or two on the organizational ladder. I'm of the belief the entire family would buy into my decision if I submitted a sound, practical and well-prepared case. If I presented my position in well thought measures, citing the positive business factors, which should culminate in a logical decision. Oh for crying out loud! Listen to me! I'm discussing this as though a state senator would when sponsoring a bill, about to be hash out on the floor, while pushing for approval. The problem here is I'm the one struggling with the decision, not the family. I don't know if I'm willing to leave my family members behind, or if I even want to leave the area, I've grown so fond of. I don't even know if I want the responsibility of the position. In that case, I don't know if it would be fair to the company to accept a position I myself am not sold on. This is the Chevy Corvette scenario revisited!

Let's look at the facts; the money would be great and would absolutely enhance all of our financials, in every area. To be honest, the money is not a huge factor in my decision, though it remains a clear positive. I know it would be a blessing for Kelly to be closer to some of her favorite family members on the Webster side. The Cleveland Indians would be in our back yard and a trip to see the Mud Hens is only an hour plus ride on the turnpike. My family still has a presence in the general Toledo area; these are all huge pluses. I guess I can hash this out six ways from Sunday, but the fact of the matter is I need to decide what I would like to do. Do I really want to accept this position? Do I really want to prioritize moving up a corporate ladder again? After all I'm only 49 and have a good fifteen plus years remaining in my working career, wherever that may be. The good news is I don't have any position or current standing in the organization. I don't have to worry about stepping on anyone's "influential" toes. This is a free shot, either take a great offer, or stay where I am happy and doing well.

Kelly and I have been discussing the move option for the past hour, and debating the pros and cons. The conversation has been an on again, off again conversation for about ten days now. I was told the company wanted an answer by the end of the month. I suspect if I was really on board, I would have accepted this generous offer by now. As well, I sense the company has already determined there is hesitation on my part, given my lack of response. It seems to me I am looking for reasons to say no, and just graciously decline.

Clearly, there will be no resolve reached tonight. It is getting late and time to retire another blessed day with Jesus and give thanks for His unconditional love. I will take the weight of this decision to Him and ask for guidance. I am honestly at a stalemate to accept or decline this offer. I need gentle but specific coaching on this issue. As I pray, I ask Jesus to clear my mind and give me the peace I need to listen for His direction. I truly hope to awaken refreshed and in positive light, with an inspired heart prepared to go forward with confidence in my decision.

Unfortunately, I tossed and turned for over an hour and was now nearly fully awake. I went down stairs and turned on the TV, and surfed the channels until I found an *easy listening* music station. Perhaps this would calm me so I could return to bed. All that accomplished was to burn another hour and a half of precious sleep time. By now it was about 12:30 AM and in defeat I returned upstairs to bed. All I know is 5:45 AM is going to come awfully early this morning. Lord help me. I finally fell asleep somewhere just before 2 AM.

It's now 5:45 and the alarm is going off like a powder keg. If I slept more than an hour and a half at one stretch, I'd be surprised. Just the same, somehow, I feel great. I don't know exactly how I came to this conclusion, but I simply decided to decline the rather generous offer tendered by my previous employer.

Last night, I took the burden of my move to Jesus. Did I hear from Him? Perhaps I did. I certainly did not receive a poem of any type, but I'm going forward with my decision. My former organization had always been good to me and I appreciate the chance to re-up, despite being several years absent from their employment. But my fondest appreciation is and always will be for Jesus and His never-ending guiding spirit. He continually reminds and supports me to seek my fondest passions. In my heart of hearts I have confirmed those deepest loves lie with family, friends, church and the beauty of the balance of those wonderful factors. This amazing blend simply allows me to experience a blessed and joyous life. No riches or position could ever compare to the blessings of the life I have experienced here in the

Carolinas. I honestly feel Jesus knew I could search my heart and be true to my passions. You also may have noticed I referred to my move as a *burden*; I'm sure Jesus did.

After officially declining the offer, Kelly asked how the company took my decision. I told her I detected some level of disappointment. I still had the business knowledge, given my position managing the industrial tool and equipment arm at the nursery. I was still as capable to step back in, despite the 13-year absence. Frankly there was more emphasis on their appreciation for my honesty in me turning down what was a very generous package. All I can say is thank you Jesus for calming my being and wiping my eyes free of the distractions which had been blinding me from seeing my blessings here. As I've come to trust Him, I was no obstacle for His ever-able abilities.

That evening after an enjoyable dinner with Kelly (roast pork tenderloin and baked asparagus) and our nightly walk topped with some heart soothing conversation, I did hear for our Lord. His words for me were clear; listen to your heart.

As worries linger, and questions loom
Pause from toil, release all pain
Last night we went from room to room
Your spirit trusted I would sustain

Your soul now still, your mind at rest
My calming peace cloaked overhead
I shined a light to seek what's best
Then your decision was calmly said

I know your heart will beat with poise
I've taught it well to fend your fear
And guide your ears to filter noise
Then wisely choose in moments clear

I've come to realize; honesty is the shortest road to a peaceful mind. Truthfulness will table issues and concerns, which must be recognized and addressed. Nevertheless, in all this righteousness, there is freedom; a cleansing of the heart in knowing a decision was made based on weighing all factors. In the guidance of Jesus, clarity is provided. We receive the ability to seek answers, which we cannot easily find on our own. In donning His armor, we acquire the Lord's strength to consider all factors and decide wisely.

Age 50

Faith Horizon Church Picnic

1997

It has been nearly five years since we planned a church picnic. Many wonderful events and happenings have occurred since our last one. We've also grown tremendously in membership, largely due to our increase in the young adults who have chosen to raise their families our area. We have added a new building to our campus, to accommodate our welcomed growth. Our modern much needed new building has a large nursery, eight classrooms complete with current electronic amenities, and a fenced outdoor playscape for the kids.

Given a good majority of our growth is thirty somethings or younger, our footprint in the community holds strong promise our presence will remain vibrant for decades to come. Much of that growth can be attributed to the addition of Pastor Joshua Gains. Pastor

Josh is in his mid-late thirties and was brought on as assistant to Pastor Stan about two years ago. We started our search for another pastor a few years back, by the insistence of our now senior Pastor Stanley Wilkerson. Pastor Stan has been with our church since its inception twenty-three years ago, and is looking to step back a bit and do some traveling with Mrs. Wilkerson. Under the title of Pastor of family services, Pastor Josh has been a tremendous blessing to Stan and our entire congregation. His approach in reaching our younger generation is visibly evident. The love and presence of our Lord clearly resonates in his heart, as he preaches the grace of Jesus. Josh is a gem of a guy and we all deeply love and appreciate him.

Every church prays for an influx of younger people, to support growth and provide the hope of future stability. Being blessed with the arrival of younger Christians, our activities committee decided we are long overdue for a church picnic. Our intention is to welcome these young families and their children. The picnic will encourage our entire church family to enjoy and fellowship together and better get to know each other.

Once the ladies Wednesday night bible study group heard about the picnic, a number of us men quickly got drafted into active duty. Several of our names were tabled to *volunteer* for this joyous event; before long all in favor of Dan Lowe as picnic chairman say "aye" was suggested by my lovely and thoughtful wife. Wow, what a blessing (I think) to be unanimously selected for such an important and *pleasurable* position. In similar fashion Jake Lloyd, owner of a local bakery, was nominated as the food chairman, in large thanks to wife and co-bakery owner Cilla Lloyd. To that food committee, add Walter and Earl Lynch. Walt you may recall is a local grocery store owner. He is getting on a bit in age and he has recently partnered with his nephew Earl to manage the store. Renay (Earl's considerate wife) was kind enough to add Walt and Earl to the list of volunteers. Earl is one of our young energetic church members, and very active in our youth ministry. Autumn Marsh along with her husband Tyler, are a young couple who opened a local florist. They will provide center pieces for the picnic tables, as well as donate floral arrangements for the service which will precede the picnic. Before those and other duties get worked out, we need to select a location worthy of hosting our blessed event.

Within a couple of weeks, our committee is forming into a nice mix of our young vibrant members, along with some of our slightly more *experienced* folks; such as me. At fifty, rather than saying *older*, I look for clever ways of suggesting I've celebrated a few more birthdays than many in our congregation. In truth, I love our young crowd and feel blessed to be working with them as we plan out the event.

As the chairman of the picnic, it is my responsibility to offer several potential sites for group committee approval. Our property stretches over several acres, but recent additions have reduced our ability to host events requiring a large space. There is a large park maintained by the county, which is a possibility. City Park which is right in the heart of town is also on my list. Several local businesses have abundant amounts of land and space, adjacent to their business. Many of these companies have hosted appreciation events for their customers and employees. These options and others should provide several choice locations for committee approval.

Plans for the picnic took shape and great progress was reported at every meeting. Food, flowers, games and entertainment, everything was moving in the splendid guidance of the Lord. Unfortunately progress was advancing in every area but one... picnic location!

One by one, each possible picnic site fell by the wayside. The county park is thirty miles from the church and was dismissed as logistically unfavorable. City Park fell from consideration, once we learned of the sea of permits which would need to be secured, and the hoops which we would have had to jump through. Every business which had ample land and offered favorable facilities, was dismissed one after another. A car dealership was preparing for expansion and unable to offer space. Other businesses either had events that weekend or cited insurance concerns and respectfully declined. I was one of the few people who had good news to report. Nonetheless, the committee stayed positive and Jesus kept my head high and a smile on my face. I assured the group I would leave no opportunity unchecked, and I was fully confident I would soon be able to offer one if not two good suggestions for approval.

The following evening Dana stopped by for dinner. During dessert, Kelly, Brandon, Dana, and I chatted about the picnic. We tabled our thoughts on possible locations, and made a concerted effort to think outside the box in our suggestions. We considered the local high school, even other churches which had large tracts of land, but nothing seemed to scream out "here I am"! Many locations were too small, or there were limited utilities to accommodate our large crowd.... By most accounts we're expecting upwards of three hundred people could attend. One idea after another was being discarded. Like a little leaguer facing the likes of Nolan Ryan, we struck out with each suggestion. Despite my trust in Jesus, knowing He will never give us too much to handle, I (for the first time) was beginning to worry. The evening passed and the ideas dried up. Time for Dana to give out good night hugs to all of us, and for our group to hit the hay.

After brushing and getting ready for bed, Kelly and I tossed out a couple of fleeting ideas. She then suggested the possibility of utilizing the acreage behind the nursery where I work. The area is kept neat and the grounds are cut. Several picnic tables are nicely arranged and offer a pleasant break area for our yard staff. The remains of an old softball diamond are nestled off to the side, and from what I've observed, it's still playable. A few years back, as part of a customer appreciation week, Travis Betts built the diamond, and hosted a tournament for his vendors. On a couple of occasions, I've seen some of the employees shagging flies during lunch time. I think with a little TLC, the back acreage of our facility may just be the answer to our prayers. No question it would take some work, but our church volunteers and I suspect some of our nursery employees, would willingly pitch in and bring the grounds up to speed. We'll pray on this possibility and close the day on a positive note. I will for sure speak to Travis about this possibility, first thing in the morning.

Kelly and I tucked in, said our prayers, and turned off the lights. I took a deep sigh and closed the day in peace, leaving the concerns of the church location to Jesus. I'm bushed and the promise of tomorrow will bring another exciting day. Time to enjoy this moment in trust Jesus will keep watch over me and my family as we sleep. Before too long, as I slept, Jesus shared His thoughts and expressed His wisdom on the picnic...

Do not fret where to meet
Father's lands are vast
Roads are plenty
Streets are many
You have a worthy cast
To meet just up the street

Your friend possesses ample ground
So look no further than to him
His place has land
His space is grand
Hearts will fill to the brim
I'll keep the picnic safe and sound

My morning started out with me sporting my huge signature smile, and offering a gracious thank you to Jesus for a good night's sleep. I guess Kelly suggestion was right. The ample grounds behind the nursery seem to be Jesus's choice as well. I will get with *him* first thing; I'm sure Travis will be fine with the suggestion and (knowing his giving heart) even offer to help in getting the place ready for June 22nd. We'll need to secure plenty more tables, but there is ample room to set up the kid's games and utilities which will allow for food preparations. After all my worry and concern, I think this is what is referred to as "problem solved"!

I left the house and headed to work on one of the most beautiful Carolina mornings I've ever experienced. Perfect weather and a great day on tap... even the sluggish commute which was beginning to increase everyone's drive time, dared not dampen my spirits, as I slowly inch closer to the nursery. I kept a confident smile peacefully displayed on my face, in anticipation of Travis supporting our picnic request.

I am now only a quarter of a mile from work and I am quickly coming to the realization that our driving delays are related to slow traffic emanating for our nursery. As I inched nearer and nearer to work, I could see very slow-moving construction equipment going in and out of our grounds. This is a very odd situation. Typically large slow-moving vehicles are either delivering goods to the nursery in the form of sand or rock, or large pieces of equipment for us to sell on our equipment lot. Neither of these scenarios are the cause of the delay.

Finally arriving at work, after briefly stopping in at my office, I strolled out back to take a look. I quickly discovered the reason for the slow commute. To my surprise (and dismay) I discovered our lovely green back lot and presumed future site for our church picnic, has morphed into a staging area for a new subdivision being built just beyond our back-property line. I certainly was aware of the upcoming construction, but had no idea the construction vehicles would be utilizing our property, and our street entrance for this project.

After a long conversation with Travis, it seems he and Dave Langley tendered an agreement with the construction company for the use of our road access to the highway for today only. Since their portable office and many of their construction vehicles will be housed in the back part of the subdivision, we are allowing the use of our entrances to bring in their equipment, which seems to be arriving in near army convoy fashion. Travis is also allowing the construction company the use of some of our cleared areas for the first few months of their start up. In exchange for our courtesies, we will be receiving some landscaping opportunities as each phase opens up over the next few years. This is certainly a great opportunity for the nursery, but our picnic chances have come to a screeching halt.

Later that day at dinner, I commiserated with Kelly about the lost opportunity she suggested in the nursery hosting the picnic. "Keep praying for guidance Dan" she suggested. The back lot sounded good, but obviously it was not the right fit for the picnic", Kelly concluded. She's right; the correct site for us is out there... we just need to find it.

Overnight I tossed and turned while struggling with our dilemma. Exhausted by my unrelinquished worries, I finally fell to sleep. Eventually calm came over me; I know this feeling, I'm about to receive His words...

As morning broke, I was somewhat perplexed. For the first time ever I received the same words of guidance from Jesus as I received the night before. I mean the exact same word for word dream! I was certain the dream was regarding our nursery property and that Travis would be all for the idea. But our work property is no longer available to be a gracious host. I am at a loss with the entire situation. I think I will talk to Travis specifically about the picnic, just to see if by chance anything comes to light.

After opening the office, and addressing some pressing matters, with coffee mug in hand, I strolled over to the nursery office, to take my morning break. I found Travis outside his office, sitting on a lawn chair, sipping on his sweet tea, observing day two of the construction site, now nestled nicely on our *not to be enjoyed* church picnic area…. (Opps, getting a bit in the flesh, sorry). "Care for some company", I asked? "Pull up a lawn chair and take a load off", Travis courteously replied. "Travis", I quickly began, "I am in charge of looking for a site for our church picnic. Long story short, we exhausted every reasonable possibility. We even thought to ask about using the back lot of the nursery", I suggested while pointing in that direction. "Obviously that possibility is no longer an option. Still, I feel compelled to ask for your advice as to where the picnic can be held", I concluded, hoping he wouldn't as for details. "Well Danny my friend, I'm glad you did", Travis quickly replied, as my attention perked. "How many people will be coming and when is the event"? He asked. I quickly responded to both questions. "I think my ranch would be the perfect location", suggested Travis with a huge grin. Now I knew he had some property, but frankly I know little about it; I'm not even sure where his land is located. As it turns out, Travis has nearly forty acres. He has all kinds of farm animals, which can easily be turned into a petting farm for the kids. He has a large barn, which has hosted square dancing events in the past. Travis's barn can easily can convert into a chapel for our morning service, (who wouldn't mind sitting on a bale of hay as a make shift pew)? He has a big outdoor cooking area and lots of room for games, activities, and fellowship. Best of all, Travis's farm is right down from the road from the nursery and only about ten or twelve miles from our church. Who Knew! We have finally found the location for our picnic; it is more than ample... it is perfect!

After sharing the news with Kelly and the picnic committee, they unanimously agreed on the site. I was as relieved as the Whitehouse turkey, receiving his reprieve on Thanksgiving. That night, I'm sure Jesus felt my relief, while chilling with me on the park bench of course. He then quietly uttered these restful assurances ...

Look no further than to him
To meet just up the street
His place has land
His space is grand
Hearts will fill to the brim

These were lines from the dream Jesus shared with me not once but twice earlier this week. It was clear Travis was somehow key in facilitating the picnic, but I didn't understand he would generously offer his ranch to host our event. I guess this is why Jesus wants us to fellowship and support one another. Once I had conversation with Travis, all became clear. But before the dream concluded, there was a pause in the message I received form Jesus. Not sure for how long, but long enough to indicate He had more to say. This is what Jesus said.

Perhaps he too will fill to the brim
And too each Sunday again and again

Interesting. Certainly Travis will be present at our picnic. I suspect he will see all the smiling faces he helped create with his generosity. I know he loves to eat, so Travis will get a hearty taste of the great dishes and desserts our congregation has to offer. Of more importance I hope he takes to heart the fellowship, kindness, and love our church will no doubt extend to him again and again over the course of the day. Jesus seems to be suggesting Travis will fill to the brim as we will.

I look forward to working with my friend Travis Betts each day of the week at the nursery. I pray I will also see him each Sunday as well, in praise of Jesus. Amen!

Age 51

Kelly's 50th Birthday Bash

1998

My fiftieth birthday was not much different than my forty ninth. That was fine with me. Yes, there was the obligatory over the hill office luncheon complete with gag gifts, black balloons and so forth. Someone insisted on hanging a cane over the back of my chair, but since cake was involved, it was all good. All the attention was not necessary, but certainly I appreciate everyone's efforts.

At home it was a totally different story. Kelly and I both knew better than she attempting a surprise fiftieth birthday for me. We settled for a nice celebration at home with family. I did get a nice surprise; since Kelly treated me to a steak dinner at the country club the

Saturday after my actual birthday. We enjoyed a table for two, just she and me and a bottle of the bubbly, to toast my half century of mortality. What a gem she is.

For Kelly though, it will be different. As often mentioned, the Websters celebrate everything in a big way. Life to them in general is a worth celebrating... can't argue that. The mile stone of fifty years for the likes for their daughter will undoubtedly mark the largest birthday gathering in Webster history. This is their beloved Kelly and this gathering will be one for the record books. Kelly is an August baby, so the big event will be outdoors, held at her Aunt Carla's house. Kelly's dad, Phil, has two brothers; Jesse and Vic. The baby of the group is his sister and party host, Carla. Carla is only sixty-five, not a whole lot older than us. She and husband Bob have a beautiful home on Lake Erie. Their place is impressively large; with a huge pavilion know for accommodating many Webster holiday extravaganzas. Having Kelly's fiftieth was a given; not a surprise party per say, but a surprise or two is likely to enter into the picture, at some point during the festivities.

Much of the planning is being done by Carla and Bob, along with their kids, Tia, Anna and Robbie. Kelly's mom and her brother Ron, make up the rest of the planning team. Kelly is as special to the family as she is to me; no doubt will be a memorable occasion. I suspect we will enjoy an all-day event, extending well into the evening hours. Anyone will be welcome to spend the night at the beach house, located to the right of their home on this remarkable compound. Kelly's Uncle Bob is a contractor and the beach house is basically another living quarters. It's a smartly built two story, with a kitchen, den, powder room and a game room downstairs. Upstairs there is a full bath, with bunking quarters for about a dozen people. An outdoor changing and shower room was recently added, for those who want to partake in lake activities.

As we neared the party day, I asked Kelly how she felt about turning fifty. I posed the typical questions one does, when trying to pry out a response about getting older...

Do you feel like you are getting older?
Do you wonder where have the years gone?
Do you think about the things which you could do in your twenties, but struggle to do now?

You know, all the classic stuff one may reminisce about when hitting this wonderful milestone. She casually looked at me with a smile and a wink. The ever-present sparkle glittered from her eyes as she replied. "No, no and no".

I just shook my head. This lovely creation of the Lord does not have a superficial bone in her entire being. Many people may reply by answering no, but few can be as convincing as she, even when answering with single word responses.

The party committee is nicely putting things in place and the first of the surprises is beginning to take shape. When Kelly was a little girl, from K to the fifth grade, she had a wonderful friend by the name of Wendy Hiller. She and Wendy were inseparable. The family shared some pictures from the Webster family photo album and they looked very much like sisters. There certainly were differences in their appearance, but from a distance, other than Wendy being a couple of inches taller, they absolutely looked like family. After the fifth grade, Wendy moved to PA. Shortly after that she and her family moved to Texas and eventually Kelly lost track of Wendy. Time and distance took its toll, and ultimately separated these two dear friends. The girls grew up and inevitably the pen pal letters came to an end. The memory of the endless times the girls spent with one another, gave Carla an idea. She decided to look Wendy up. Being fifteen when Kelly was born, Carla had clear recollections of Wendy and Kelly as devoted friends. It was Carla's detective work and persistence that opened up the doors to reunite these two dear friends after nearly forty years of separation.

The next day, Carla got working on this wonderful reunion. Carla had a friend, who had a friend that new someone that… well anyway she was eventually led to a small town in Texas where Wendy and her family first relocated. She then discovered Wendy had married and the couple formed a business in Waco. Carla got the number of their establishment and she placed her call. After some memory joggling, Wendy seemed recall to Kelly's Aunt Carla; she certainly had no problem remembering her dear friend Kelly. Sadly, Wendy shared that both her parents had left us; her Mom recently died after a long illness, and her dad had died several years back, from cancer when he was only in his mid-forties. Her family was spread all over the country and was sparse in remaining living members. Add to that, she and her husband Norm had recently divorced. They were still working together as business partners, until they could sort out the financial details of splitting the business. The most incredible part of the conversation was the timing of the communication. Wendy was feeling the weight of life bearing down on her. She was struggling with her faith, given all the difficulties which piled on her at one time; her mom's death, her divorce, and turning fifty. Yes, the girl's birthdays were just two days apart; Kelly is on the tenth, Wendy's on the twelfth. Jesus clearly planted the idea for Carla to reunite this precious child hood friendship.

When Carla disclosed the content of the conversation she had with Wendy, they realized two wonderful things were happening. First Kelly will be getting a surprise visit from a dear friend, forty years separated. Secondly and of more importance, her inseparable mate from years past who is struggling on multiple fronts and now finding herself fifty and alone, thinking the world has tossed her aside, will get a reunion of a lifetime. The girls will celebrate their fiftieth together, and Kelly will be totally floored when she finds out.

The next day, Wendy again called Carla. Her ex graciously agreed to man the business for the weekend. Wendy booked a flight and Carla will pick her up at Cleveland Municipal Airport, and host her stay for this festive occasion. The good news is Kelly agreed to stay away from the party site. Given she is the *lady of the hour*; we didn't want her to see the decorations, or be saddled with any set up duties. This at least is our excuse, and an easy sell to keep her away and assure Wendy's visit will be a complete surprise. What a blessing this will be for all of us; for Wendy who desperately needs fellowship and family lovin,' and for Kelly who will have a surprise reunion of a lifetime.

As I stretched in bed, the night before the big day, I gave thanks for everything, and asked Jesus to bless the wonderful event set for tomorrow. I gave Kelly a kiss and stated, "tomorrows your big day, Kel". I was looking to get her final thoughts, as a person about to turn fifty years old. "It will be a wonderful day", she countered. "I will be lucky enough to be with all the people in my life that mean the most to me. There are many people in the world who are unable to make that statement. I am fortunate and blessed beyond words", she concluded. With that sentiment shared, while well said and spot on, she has no idea what additional blessing she soon will be receiving.

Planning big events can be taxing and tiring, but so totally worth the effort. When everything finally falls in place, a deep breath can be taken by everyone. Feelings of both relief and satisfaction will no doubt settle our collective souls. God bless Carla for everything, the planning, her hospitality of hosting, and mostly for the understanding and loving compassion she is extending to Wendy. This celebration will mean everything to these two dear friends. This may be one of the more special days I have ever spent with Kelly. God is so good. After prayers and a good night kiss, I quickly fell asleep.

I slept soundly and woke up refreshed. I looked at the clock and it was only 5:15 AM. Given Kelly's big day is upon us, and the strong likelihood the day's events will go into the late evening, 5:15 is entirely too early to start my day. I decided to doze back off and try to catch a few more winks, before beginning what promised to be an exciting, but long day. Before long, I fell back to sleep. I then heard this gracious and *revealing* comment from our Lord Jesus...

Do you remember
When you were a child?
When best of friends
Ran free and wild?

Untamed was your passion
To spend your hours
With your friend like a sister
Picking out flowers

Some went in vases
Some in your hair
Each one of them special
Placed gently with care

You were the rose
She was the lily
Striking a pose
Both serious and silly

But friendships like flowers
As each pedal falls
Grow apart over time
Until someone calls

But seedlings take root
Surviving each season
In a tasteful arrangement
For a special reason

My unique bouquet
The Lily and Rose
This door I will open
So never you'll close

I again woke up with my smile beaming wide; Jesus just privied me to a special bit of Kelly Lynn history. Kelly and her mate from the early years were flower lovers; true *flower girls* ten years ahead of their time.

Kelly often kept fresh cut flowers from the garden, arranged in a clear vase on the dining room table. As I went down to brew a pot of coffee, I took a rose out of the vase on the table. I trimmed the stem to a suitable length, allowing me to gently clip the rose to Kelly's hair. As I walked up the steps and entered the room, I carefully stepped with a coffee cup in each hand. In my right hand I also carried the rose, with the stem pinched between two fingers. Kelly was waking up and sitting propped up against the headboard, still under the quilt. After placing our coffees on the end tables, I carefully pinned the rose in her hair, and handed her a mirror. Over the years, I don't recall her sporting that look. Perhaps on a couple of occasions in the sixties maybe, but wearing a flower was not part of her typical appearance. She looked in the mirror displaying a smile and a nostalgic expression. I smiled back without saying a word. She still had a bit of a distant look, and I wouldn't be at all surprised if she was thinking about the days when she and Wendy wore flowers in this manner. By the way, she left the rose in her hair all morning. After her shower she placed it back in the exact place I pinned it. Occasionally I noticed her glancing in the mirror, and once striking a silly pose. It seems old habits do die hard.

As we got ready for the party, I got a call from Carla on my mobile phone. "Can you discretely pick up a few lilies from the florist?" requested Carla. "Sure, no problem", I casually replied, reasonably sure I knew why. We finished getting ready, gathered up the kids, (the lilies) and we headed over to Carla and Bob's.

On the way over, Kelly flipped down the visor and took a quick peek in the mirror. She had a pleasant smile and gently ran her forefinger across one of the pedals. "Something wrong", I asked? "No", she quickly replied. "Just thinking and reminiscing some old thoughts from way back". I let the conversation go at that. She has no clue ... this is going to be great!

We arrived at Bob and Carla's, and a good twenty-five or thirty people were already there. A number of them were taking things out to the back yard where the party will be happening. "Where's Wendy?" I quietly asked. "She's waiting in the beach house for most of the guests to arrive', whispered back Carla. The invitation asked people to be here at 2: 00 PM sharp! I'm guessing this was to keep Wendy's solitary confinement to a minimum.

By 2:15 PM we had at least fifty people in the yard. All our family, our friends the Langley's from Charlotte,

Jenny Masters Kelly's college friend, just a big happy crowd. Uncle Jesse just put two platters of burgers and dogs, on the already overflowing banquet tables. This was a buffet for a queen who just turned the wonderful age of fifty. Kelly was asked to say a few words about the gathering, before Uncle Bob said grace.

"Everyone, thank you for blessing my day in helping me share in this celebration", began Kelly. Her opening remark was the cue for Wendy to come out of the beach house. Once she came out, she was asked to firmly close the door, in an effort to get Kelly's attention. Given everyone was quietly awaiting the reunion, I think the slamming door could have been heard across the lake. As hoped, Kelly turned around to see an approaching figure; her once considered twin, Wendy Hiller. Remarkably there was still a resemblance, both natural blonds, though Wendy's cut was a bit shorter than Kelly's. The lily was dutifully place in the exact same manner as in the fifties, when they were kids. As Wendy made her way up the slight incline for the beach house, Kelly's jaw dropped. Before Kelly uttered a word, her eyes welled and tears were streaming down her cheeks. "Hey Kel l–bell ", uttered Wendy. The girls now running toward each other were locked in a hug, forty years in the making. "I missed you so much", said Wendy. Kelly, still speechless was smiling, crying and just taking in her old dear friend. "Aren't you going to finish your birthday speech?" asked Wendy. Kelly never did.

As they party got into full swing, Carla brought out an old photo album, mostly made up of pictures of the birthday girl. A montage of Kelly Lynn Webster Lowe, from bare-bottomed infant to current wife and mother of two. One picture in particular featured Wendy and Kelly, standing side by side sporting new two-wheel bikes. Both girls got them for their eight birthdays. Schwinn bikes with big fat tires, and streamers hanging from the handle grips. The girls looked like twins, but no flowers in the hair, in this shot.

Everyone gazed at the photo album and snapped one picture after another of the girls like paparazzi. Wendy then asked all of us to quietly gather around her and Kelly. "I have something for you Kelly", announced Wendy. She pulled out a framed picture from her travel bag. Wendy produced a beautiful hinged frame, which opened to feature two eight by ten glossy photos. The two beautiful photos were taken by her father. Wendy's dad worked as a photographer for the Toledo Blade. He took the shots with his 35MM work camera. These were the clearest black and white photos I have ever seen. One photo featured the girls tastefully posing with flowers in their hair while in birthday dresses. The other shot was similar, featuring the girls sticking out their tongues and crossing their eyes. With flowers perfectly in place as they were some forty years ago, little urging was needed for the birthday girls to pose for new shots, 1998 style.

Needless to say, the girls were practically inseparable most of the evening. At some point I got ahold of my birthday girl and received a big hug. "How exactly did you know about the rose in the hair thing? I don't think I ever mentioned it", she said. "Well", I said pausing. "It just kind of came to me the night before", I suggested, raising an eyebrow. "He knows everything, doesn't He"? Kelly said with a wink. "Yes, He does", I agreed.

As cake was brought out, Carla (God Bless her) tastefully included Wendy's name on the cake. It proudly stated "HAPPY 50TH, Kelly and Wendy!"

What a beautiful day the Lord gave us. What a blessing it was to meet Wendy. The hardship of losing her dad, then her mom, coupled with a recent divorce, is enough to wear down the strongest of us. At least for now those troubles can be replaced by claiming the joy of a loving reunion.

This was not a surprise 50th birthday party by nature; but it did feature one very pleasant surprise. Kelly and I both have been blessed many times by many wonderful people over the years. I would have to say this reunion of two dear friends, separated since childhood for nearly forty years, united together to celebrate their half century birthday, is the greatest gifts either one of them could receive. Reunions such as these are once in a lifetime experience. All made possible by a loving family with willing hearts, eager to bring together childhood soulmates. In this reunion Jesus has not only rekindled a friendship, but brought renewed faith and hope to Wendy.   Wendy will have trying times, but she and Jesus have this. She also has the strength of her soul sister and life time friend, to lean on when she is needed. I can assure Wendy; her friend Kelly will never lose sight of her again. She can count on that!

Age 52

Brandon's New Digs

1999

Every parent endures a series of emotions when one of their children leaves the roost. My son Brandon recently cut the umbilical housing cord this past month, joining the ranks of home ownership.

We had already been down that road twice with daughter Dana. First, went off to college, then again when she moved into her first place. Kelly handled Dana's departures far better than I. I struggled with letting her go, until I relinquished the reins of worry to Jesus's capable hands. Unwilling to echo a similar spectacle showcasing sentimental syrupy soppiness, (smiley face), this time I was mentally prepared to see Brandon move out and put his mark on the world.

Brandon had lived at home until he was nearly twenty-four. He commuted to college for four years, and continued to live at home after landing his first job. He did so in an effort to squirrel away as much money as he could, so he could buy his first starter home. We agreed, as long as he saved his money for a down payment on his own place, Kelly and I would forego charging him rent. During that time, he did hold his own fiscally. He paid his own car insurance, did his wash, and contributed in paying down part of our huge food bill; given his active participation at the dinner table. This was a nice agreement which worked for us and him. He could still save money, while bearing the burden of economic responsibility which he ultimately would need to shoulder.

Our arrangement was a good life-learning tool, but Brandon's financial skills actually developed at a much early age. His money disciplines are comparable to those of a tight-fisted banker. I recall on one occasion, his sister Dana wanted to borrow fifty dollars. It seems there was this awesome sweater, which was a must have to complete the perfect outfit, for a job interview. Brandon authored an agreement for her signature, assuring she would pay him back, no later than receipt of her second full paycheck. I don't want to suggest my son is a scrooge, but I should mention, in the past he fell victim to a few defaulted loans of five or ten dollars, curtesy of Dana. At some point, he realized many of those advances actually became gifts. Dana basically used Brandon as a personal ATM machine. However, in developing his no interest agreement, which she willingly signed; a deal would be created which they both could live with. Dana had joked she wished she could have listed Brandon as a credit reference, when it came time to purchase her first car.

Fast forward form those early days of fiscal learning, it is time for Brandon to move out and find his own place. He'd been aggressively house hunting for about two or three months, when he stumbled across the listing which ultimately became his first home. A new listing surfaced featuring a nice neat three-bedroom two bath ranch. This house was a flipper and was move in ready, complete with appliances, new everything, and situated on a plot of land a little over one acre in size. Given Brandon's natural financial savviness, he knew flippers typically are reasonable negotiators. He managed to get the house and still have enough left over to construct the small shed, needed to house his riding mower and store his soon to expand tool collection.

Moving day went pretty well, fortunately not too many nicked door jambs, and Brandon was now a proud new home owner. But again, Kelly and I still felt the ups and downs of a child moving out. Though Brandon has left the nurturing nest in favor of his own digs, he certainly has not forgotten where Mom and Dad live, particularly at dinner time. Given the appetite of an active young man such as he, coupled with the fact that Kelly possesses superior cooking skills, he certainly was no stranger to our dinner table. In fact, it took a few weeks for Kelly to break the routine of setting a place for Brandon, at his long-time spot where he donned the feed bag.

We are pleased our son has moved on to a new chapter in his life; but with both kids out of the nest, the house is echoing with emptiness. Dinnertime is so quiet, the ringing of the tinnitus in my ears has become deafening. On the positive side, Kelly and I have again realized the joy of asking "so how was your day dear", and actually have the time and focus to honestly responded. Just the same our house, while quieter, more straightened, and much more orderly, is a lonelier place. It feels heart breaking in some ways.

This empty and spacious home of ours, for the time being at least, is far too large for our day to day living. Five bedrooms, three and a half baths, great room, a game room, and a library often seemed too small when overrun by teen friends visiting our kids. Today we could easily lose one another in the roominess... for short periods of time anyway. Our thought is to hang on to the place and patiently wait for the rooms to again be filled with visiting grandchildren. Given their tireless youthful energy, I'm sure they will seemingly fill several rooms at once. Did I just say I would patiently wait for grandchildren? Dana is career oriented, single and motherhood is not even in her current vocabulary. Brandon, is in his rookie season of home ownership, and is still working to establish himself at work. As he put it, "I am standing on the bottom rungs of the corporate ladder, but I am optimistically looking upward". These scenarios leave us positioned well back in the new grandparent's line. Do you recall when younger, we would ask to "take cuts" in line? If we arrived late to a show or some event, and the line to the box office traveled down the block and around the corner, one would cruise the line looking for a friend, willing to give them *cuts*. I wish there was a grandparent's line. I would ask anyone and everyone to cut in. Great concept, but I'm not holding my breath. It's again time to simply realize each day is a gift, and to embrace our moments as they unfold. Allow time to pass, and God willing one day that glorious moment will arrive, when one of our children will announce, "Dad, you're going to be a Grandpa"! So... patient I'll be.

So, Brandon, Kelly and I discussed his new place, and the furnishings in this cozy dwelling. The typical array of orphaned furniture one would expect to find, which he best positioned in an effort to display their remaining brilliance. A nice sofa; clean, comfortable and stain free, purchased on, "My Neighbors List", is the first piece seen as you enter the through front door. The recliner in the corner compliments the sofa and offers a warm and welcoming look, is curtesy of Kelly. A win / win for Brandon and Kelly, he gets a nice chair, she creates the opportunity to buy a new one. This is the unwritten rule of children blowing the coop; as they move, so goes their bed and their bedroom furniture. Again, Kelly hits pay dirt, this time it's an entire room to furnish, while creating yet another guest room, begging for overnight company.

At his new home, Brandon converted one of his bedrooms into an office. The room is furnished with the table from his old bedroom, his computer and a file cabinet which I willingly surrendered from our garage. The third bedroom is his guest room, or better said his future guest room. At this point the amenities are a bit lacking for an overnight guest. Visitors better bring a sleeping bag, or willing to bunk on the living room sofa. Certainly, Brandon has a way to go before completing his furnishing tasks. No rush, he has plenty of time to do so. Still, from my fatherly perspective, I can't wait until one of the bedrooms will happily become a nursery.

Architecturally speaking, Brandon's home is in fact very nice both inside and out. Prior to moving in all of the rooms received a fresh coat of off-white paint. As a new home owner, he started with a clean canvas, enabling his design ideas to travel in any desired direction. He had already painted his living room and his bedroom in shades of grey and tan respectively, both of which complement the oak hardwoods. A few days after the move, I stopped by and asked if he needed a hand with anything. Five minutes later I was stirring a can of autumn tan paint, in preparation to roll a fresh coat on the guest room walls. Brandon was in his office with a can of Glacier Grey, in preparation to tackle that room.

We chatted back and forth a bit, as we both dutifully worked on our projects. When we hit moments of silence, I smiled in thought, wondering when I may again be asked to help change the color from tan to either a shade of baby blue or perhaps a pastel pink. This again leads to thoughts of fantasizing about being a grandpa. I'm not one to dwell in the past, and I don't want to place too much thought on the future. I'd rather stay in the present, enjoy the rewards of the moment, and relish life "in real time", in the presence of Jesus.

As I was rolling the final wall, I felt a peaceful easiness enveloping my demeanor. I know this feeling very well, as it invites an ear to ear smile on my face. The senses seem to unite in one common direction. My eyes concentrate on my task, but my work became effortless. The smell of latex interior paint becomes nonexistent. My hearing closes off all sound, as I enter into the *perfect silence*. Over the years though, I've realized the incoming message may be something I need to hear, rather than something I want to hear.

In secret I have arranged all things
No eyes shall see my sacred plan
Have strength in Me, hold firm My hand
Embrace what this day brings

Though riches wait beyond each door
Impatience tends to rush your mind
To hasten thoughts ahead in time
So future gifts, would now be yours

Accept each moment as they come
The present is my daily gift
Let no wonders stray or drift
Or exit with the setting sun

But dawn shall call bold and bright
Filled with joy and teemed in hope
Rest in Me and don My yoke
All comes to pass, when time is right

The Lord reminded me I made the moment about myself. My son is starting a new chapter in his life. He is excited and is rejoicing in the accomplishment of home ownership. This is a wonderful personal achievement, and a rather major one at that, in his young adulthood. It's a moment he and I should claim together and celebrate.

I've now completed the final wall and it is time for me to put down the roller and proudly walk into the room where Brandon is working. With arms open and stretched as far as I can spread them, I give him a smile and a big fatherly hug. No words need be exchanged. Brandon and I developed this greeting a few years back. In short, it simply means "I love you".

Age 54

Ron and His Girls

2001

My brother-in-law Ron Webster is a very special man. Ron was my first friend at college. I had a connection with him from the first time we met. More than a great friend and a fantastic brother-in-law; Ron is a brother to me.

Ron recently celebrated his twenty-fifth wedding anniversary with his bride Susan. They met at the office where they both were employed. Shortly after Susan was hired, a whirlwind romance began to unfold. A love at first sight magical meeting according to Ron; and I must agree he and Susie are a perfect fit. Over the years, they have been blessed with three lovely daughters, Lake 19, Brooke 16, and Spring is 13. Yikes, college for three girls, three weddings to finance, and all the up and down joys of dating, which teenage girls face.

From Ron's perspective, he wouldn't have it any other way.

I recently got a taste of parenting multiple girls when the three of them visited for ten days. Ron and Susie took an Alaskan cruise; a twenty-fifth wedding anniversary present from Susie's parents. This gave Kelly, Dana, and I the opportunity to invite Ron's three princesses to stay at our home in South Carolina. Brandon was on a two week back pack trip in the Appalachian's with his outdoor group. This enabled me to get a dose of Ron's existence plus one daughter, my Dana. Basically, my home became a slumber party, sorority house, sisterhood of Hallmark movies gathering spot.

During the ongoing movie marathon, ice cream gorging bonding time, I did receive a few breaks from all the female festivities. Dana took the girls to the mall for a day of shopping and treated them to lunch. Kelly surprised all four girls with tickets to a Back-Street Boys concert in Charlotte. Spring enjoyed the concert more than any of them. Spring is actually her middle name. Given Ron and Sue were stopping at three children, Springs first name is Ronna. No Ron Jr. for them so Ronna was as close as they could come.

After enduring yesterday's late evening with the concert, the girls all slept in and planned a simple restful day around the house. Dana grilled some brunch for the girls and they all laughed and chatted while sprawling on lawn furniture on the patio, beneath a clear blue Carolina sky.

As evening arrived, we were back outdoors and it was my turn to man the grill. While prepping the charcoal and waiting for the pizza dough to rise, I reminisce about my longtime friend Ron Webster. Ron remains a close confidant, despite the distance which separates us. My thoughts of Ron go back to the day I met him. Two guitar players away from home for the first time attempting to establish their adult identity. The greater fortune of that friendship was when he introduced me to his sister, my lovely wife to be Kelly Lynn Webster. In my fifty-four or so years of life, through fellowship and meeting untold numbers of people, Ron and Kelly are easily two most incredible beings the Lord has graced me to become acquainted.

As I look back on my memorable days in college; the football weekends, the symphony band concerts, the day trips with friends to cites around town, pep rallies and parties, even Spring Breaks, clearly without any question, my fondest memories were gigging with the Webster kids on and around campus. We'd then critique our evening at a coffee shop afterwards. Not so much to better our performance, but just to joke, share chat and enjoy our special friendship. The Lord connected me to these amazing beings and I am forever grateful.

As I direct my thoughts back to my pizza making duties, I casually observe the relationship further blossoming, between Ron's three girls and my Dana and Kelly. Given we moved from Ohio before Lake (Ron's eldest) was born; the girls have a lifetime of history to learn and catch up on. In typical Webster fashion, the girls are approachable and talkative and more than will to share conversation. So, there they are; the five of them, Ron's three, Kelly and Dana, all in ponytails and flip-flops, laughing and joking and calling out their pizza orders, as I write down their topping requests. Enjoying a nice dinner uptown is great, and concerts are exciting, but nothing says joy and happiness, like hearts being blessed in friendship and relaxing conversation. As when in college, the simple times like these, when people get together, often are the best. I wouldn't at all be surprised if this evening resonates most in their hearts as the week goes on.

With the last pizza now scooped from the oven, the tasty treats have been delivered to our hungry group. Everyone is enjoying their own special order. I give Brooke the award for creating the most unusual combination. Anchovies, black olives, and pineapple, hardly a typical combination, but it works for her.

As the evening continued the clock was nearing 8:00 pm. The girls took the party indoors and headed for the family room. Every one claimed their recliner or a seat of choice on the sectional, and settled in for a feel-good movie marathon. Somehow, even though these movies and very predictable in plot and outcome, they manage to toss in a twist or two, to not only satisfy the viewer, but to create the need for watching another one.

As the girls settle in to their places for movie time, I begin patio clean up. Much of the food and glasses were bussed in by the girls so my duty will be quick and easy. I am more than happy to attend to my pizza eating, movie loving, soon to be brownie devouring group of Webster girls.

After the movie ended and the eyes were dried, we all went out on the deck and star gazed amid quiet conversation. The Webster girls were very grateful for the week Dana and Kelly put together, and continually thanked Kelly and me for opening up our home to them. Soon, they all began to speak about their mom and dad. They each shared wonderful heartwarming stories about their mom. Despite being a department manager at the office, Susie never missed a game, event, or play at school. You parents know the near impossible juggling acts which regularly surface, when work and school schedules clash…. And with three girls no less. But Susie is a master and the girls recognize and appreciate her loving and valiant efforts when it comes to her girls. As working parents, Susie and Ron have demonstrated respect for each other, both work schedule wise and personally at home in their relationship. When respect is demonstrated as an important virtue at home, children will observe and adopt that practice, then exude that nature to those they encounter in life. Ron and Susie are preparing three stellar young women to take their place in the world, and those fortunate to be in their acquaintance will be better for it.

As the evening wore on the eyelids got heavy. The conversation slowed as a contagious cycle of yawns circled through the group. Kelly recommended we call it a night and there was no opposition to her suggestion. It was time to take it back indoors and let our contingent of princesses head off to bed.

As I journaled, Kelly was beaming about the wonderful conversation and togetherness, which the girls were sharing. Tomorrow is Sunday and Dana is spending the night here. After church, Dana is taking the girls to the amusement park. Closing my journal, I give thanks for the graces of the day. I thank God for the blessing of opening our home to Ron and Susie's three beautiful daughters. They have brought a special elation and warmth into our home.

As I began to drift off into dreamland, I find myself in our back yard. I spot a bench and predictably sit on the far-right side. The setting however is hardly our back yard, but more resembles the center garden on campus from my college days. You know how dreams go when it comes to accuracy, but OK it's my back yard in the dream anyway.   Despite that twist in detail, Jesus's thoughts are quite clear and visually accurate…

May the lands be watered
So My plantings can grow
My Spring soaks the ground
My Brooke tends to flow
My Lake fed by rivers
Spreads joy as she grows
My three girls of water
Will reap what they sow

Each spirit unique
Their hearts rarely sad
How warmly they speak
Of their mom and dad
Respect from their mouths
 Is clearly expressed
As hearts are spoken
Upon evenings rest

Embrace them gently
Allow them to voice
Each worry and trouble
To seek a clear choice
In quirk and demeanor
Each one needs her space
My light creates vision
So she'll take her place

As I greeted the morning, I woke to clear understanding. Jesus gave me incite as to how we relate to one another and in turn shape the world. I look at Ron and Susie's three lovely daughters. These fortunate girls, from day one was parented by two special people, each of whom took the time to instill the virtue of respect to each of them. These kids will embrace those teachings as they mature into adulthood, and no doubt demonstrate compassionate values to those they encounter.

Today is a beautiful sunny South Carolina day; blue sky, fleecy clouds, and a good dash of south eastern humidity. This is a perfect day for the girls to take in the amusement park rides, the water park and all the food they can stomach (so to speak). At my age, better them than me, but one thing is for sure; my daughter Dana, accompanied by her three dear cousins, will receive this glorious day, and enjoy family fellowship. They'll adore each jubilant moment, embrace each cork screw turn, exalt in the drenching water park rapids, and somehow find bliss in a near ninety degree drop of a coaster at one hundred miles per hour. Each of these experiences will be shared together as they revel in the moment leaving no joy unclaimed.

These four girls have learned to seek and harness every happy moment which is available to them. There is elation and celebration around every turn. They have learned to rely on Jesus to guide them through the fear and worry which also can inhabit those same turns. Fortunately for them they learned Jesus's faithful guidance is there for the asking. His relief is a reminder to all who still struggle with the burden of fear and worry; it's never too late to ask for His strength.

As for me, this week Kelly and I are the proud parents of four lovely girls. To proudly quote my good friend and *brother* Ron Webster, "I wouldn't have it any other way".

Age 55

An Engaging Time for All

2002

Kelly and I never lose sight of how proud we are of our two kids. Brandon is 27 now, and Dana is 29. Dana graduated from college in 1995; by late that summer she began working in the fashion design industry. Dana is one of the most creative people I have ever met. She can draw, paint, build, design, and handle just about every kind of artistic challenge put before her. She reminds me so much of my dad; possessing the mind of a designer, the hands of a builder, and the desire to see a job through to a successful completion. Her skills don't stop there; she can sell, manage, and has perform well at every corporate position placed before her. After three years at American Girl Fashions Inc. Carolina division, she continues on her way up ladder.

Dana is confident and as cool and comfortable in her skin as her mother. She has no problem speaking up and voicing her opinion. Not in an obnoxious "blow your own horn" manner, but professionally and within appropriate company guidelines. Her ideas and drive, coupled with an insatiable appetite to participate in corporate growth, has fast-tracked her through several corporate departments.

Given we all survived Y2K, companies could again focus on their go forward plans. American Girl Fashion (AGF) was looking to increase their footprint in the fashion industry. Based in western S. Carolina, their location offered available acreage to satisfy their desire to physically grow. After land was secured, AGF contracted a building company for their expansion. Design engineers were brought in since both the office and the manufacturing mill were slated for expansion. It was determined two design teams be created to meet AGF's needs. One team will be tasked to design the office expansion, the other to address the needs of the mill. The teams were made up form people from both AGF and from the building company. Dana was selected to participate in the five-person office design team. Over the weeks to follow, the two teams would occasionally meet to compare notes, and make certain both expansions were progressing positively as the project went forward.

The project manager is a young man by the name of Eric O'Shea. Despite his youthful age of 31, Eric brings much experience and is a proven leader. Eric's job was to coordinate the entire operation and make sure the needs of both builds were met and progressing at a harmonious rate. Eric is a skilled tradesman; a third-generation builder, and educated in architectural construction and design. He is a tall, strapping, handsome Irish lad originally from Boston, though little of his New England accent remains after his move south. Eric is a superb communicator and just the right person to keep both teams on track for success.

During the initial joint design meeting, long before ground was broken, the two teams reviewed the design prints together. The prints were created by the builder based on the input of AGF's initial needs for the growth they envisioned. After the meeting was opened and discussion ensued, a young design engineer spoke up concerning the size of the office space for the design team. "The print reveals very little increase in the space designated to our design team, Mr. O'Shea", voiced my concerned young Dana. "Given the existing size of the design area you are correct Miss... (Eric paused to catch the name on Dana's ID badge) Lowe. However, due to the request for expanded office space, particularly for the design department, please turn to the next print and see the second-tier design, which will be built above the current office", Eric suggested. "And by the way, it's

Eric", he said to the group along with a bit of eye contact directed at Dana. Sure enough, given the design needs voiced by AGF, the builder developed a unique terrace design, which more than doubled the existing design center. The upper terrace will alleviate the need to dig a new footing and creatively keep building costs down. This was one of the many innovative ideas which were provided by none other than the young Mr. Eric O'Shea. "Ah, I see, very nice and very creative", stated my girl. And by the Way it's Dana", countered my fearless girl, with the ever-present Webster twinkle in her eye. Eric smiled; no doubt impressed with Dana's confidence and interest in the project.

As the weeks went on Dana kept Kelly and I up to speed on the happenings with the expansion. I got the details on the construction and Kelly got the details on Eric; or should I say Ric, as Dana calls him. It seems our driven little design engineer has caught the attention of the handsome Mr. O'Shea.

As the expansion progressed, meetings continued, and only manageable issues surfaced. As work went on and the expansion proceeded on schedule it seems other things were also progressing and taking shape. The business relationship between Dana and Ric was also evolving into a personal one. As construction was near completion, our beautiful daughter and her handsome friend were regularly dating and becoming exclusive.

One evening at bedtime, Kelly said, "Dan, I think Dana and Ric are becoming quite serious". "I know Kel, they really seem close and comfortable with each other. I think Dana is a pretty good judge of character and Ric seems like a nice young man". She nodded in agreement. "Dana told me they are exclusive; I think she is falling in love with him. She hasn't said so in so many words, but I can see it in her eyes", Kelly said. I think Kelly is right. A couple of weeks ago, we had them over for a barbeque. At one point, Ric and I were on the patio tending to the ribs, while Kelly and Dana were setting the table indoors. As Ric gazed through the patio doors focusing on Dana he said, "Your daughter is incredible Mr. Lowe. She is smart, lovely, confident, and has the most beautiful eyes I've ever seen". "He said that", Kelly asked? "Yes he did, and do you know what I told him", I replied? "No, what did you say", Kelly asked pausing mid stroke while brushing her hair. "I told him that is exactly how I felt about you, when we were dating. Kelly and I shared a smile. I think we both feel it is just a matter of time before God units these two special young people together in marriage.

As I settled into bed and continued thoughts about Dana and Ric, I concluded my driven darling daughter has the spirit of her mom, the courage of a lioness, and the heart and spirit of Jesus. She is my baby girl and I couldn't be prouder of her.

My mind is now relaxed and my body is sprawled in comfort. A great day has come to an end and the promise of a wonderful new one is just an overnight away. Morning will arrive with the assurance of Jesus and His guiding light, but not before He shared this message with me...

I know your wishes
Each inner thought
Your heart's desires
Most dearly sought

The needed piece
That loving soul
The mate you long
To make you whole

No sun will set
Or bring to close
What shines in you
My budding rose

Your father's heart
Through mother's eyes
Will guide you well
Upon sun's rise

I woke up this morning smiling and embracing the joy of the moment. I am elated to the core that Jesus again blessed me with guidance and peace. Each time I receive His moving words I reflect in awe; by just how much He loves me. After hearing from Him I often verbally say, "Why are You so good to me"? After all this time I really don't know why I still pose that question; I expect no reply, and I know He just loves me without any boundaries. I guess I am simply saying thank you.

At breakfast, I shared the interesting conversation I had last night with Kelly. She reasoned that Dana and Ric clearly have something special going on. With that conclusion voiced, we couldn't be happier.

Sometime mid-morning the phone rang and the caller ID indicated Dana was on the line. "How you are my budding rose", Kelly said in greeting, citing one of the lines from last night's poem. "What did you call me", Dana asked in a slightly confused voice. "Nothing, never mind", quipped Kelly. "It's odd you said that", began Dana. "I got an early morning delivery from the florist, a dozen beautiful red roses. "The card said; *your tender touch brings every bud to bloom, love Ric"*. Dana continued, "Is that why you called me your *budding rose*; did Ric tell you he was sending flowers?" Dana questioned. "No, just a coincidence I guess, just something your dad and I were chatting about earlier", Kelly remarked.

After conversation regarding the roses concluded, Dana invited Kelly and me to join them at dinner this evening. We had tentative plans to catch a show at the cinema, but dinner with our lovely daughter and her man sounded perfect.

That evening we arrived at Elliot's Fine Steaks, just in time to see Dana and Ric being seated in the dining room. As we joined them it was clear the expressions on their faces were beaming with excitement. Elliot's is the perfect meeting place; not too loud for good conversation and excellent steaks and sea food is a guarantee. It's a comforting place to break bread and indulge in conversation such as sharing plans for an upcoming engagement and wedding perhaps? We'll soon see.

Dana looked lovely as usual, but was sporting one particular accessory which she rarely wore: evening gloves. Elliot's was a jacket and tie type place so evening gloves for the ladies was not too much out of the ordinary, but rather formal for my girl. We started conversation and began with small talk regarding the expansion at AGF. In reality I'm continually kept up to speed by my darling daughter in detail, so this conversation was clearly the undercard for the main event. Finally, I couldn't wait any longer. "Hands cold Dana", I asked pointing to her evening gloves. She and Ric glanced at each other sporting smiles which indicated we were on to their *big news*. Dana gently placed her knife and fork on the linen table cloth and with style and glamor. She dramatically extended her left arm toward the center of the table, while removing the glove with her right hand. Her delicate left hand proudly displayed a full carat diamond, round cut, tastefully set on a white gold band. "Oh, my goodness, that is lovely", exclaimed Kelly. Kelly rose and dashed around the table to hug Dana. Both girls had the waterworks streaming down their faces. Ric and I both got up and met each other half way to exchange a handshake and a hug. As we all returned to our seats, we received smiles and nods of congratulations from neighboring tables. The crowd reaction was a bit less sensational than the fervor caused by my engagement announcement at the country club thirty-five years earlier, but in my heart this one feels like a bigger blessing. My beautiful girl is going to be married. Thank you, Jesus, for graciously bringing Ric into my girl's life.

Conversation again continued at the table with Ric offering these words; "Mr. and Mrs. Lowe, you daughter is the most incredible person I have had the fortune to meet. She is amazing, beautiful, smart and fearless. It would be an honor for you to allowing me to have her hand in marriage". Our response was an overwhelming yes you may.

After giving our blessings to Ric and Dana, I had my eyes fixed on my sweet daughter. She was staring at me with a peaceful, happy and satisfied smile. Her eyes were saying "I love you Daddy" and my thoughts of her wonderful young life raced through my mind... I saw glimpses of the things she has done over her 29 years. Assisting Kelly with Brandon as nurse Dana, helping design and build her playhouse with Daryl and I, all her musical and sports interest, to graduating university and becoming a successful fashion design engineer and accomplished business person. What an absolute lovely creation the Good Lord blessed Kelly and me with. What an outstanding young man she was led to find in her life journey.

Speaking of my little rose bud, she sportingly had placed one of the dozen roses on the right side of her head, Kelly Lynn style. After sharing the announcement of her engagement, she appropriately moved the rose to the left side of her head, signifying to the world she is no longer available. No firm date has been set but they are thinking fall of 2003.

After the announcement and as we feasted on some of Elliot's beast twelve-ounce fillets, I could see the wheels already turning in Kelly's head. After all this gives her and Dana an opportunity to have a Webster family monster event of unprecedented proportions. Already being mid-September, the rest of the year will fly by beginning with Halloween; then Thanksgiving immediately followed by the glorious Christmas season, and we'll close the year with the countdown to midnight watching the ball drop in Time Square. This only leaves eight or nine months for Dana and Kelly to plan our daughter's wedding. Knowing Kelly, it will exceed the bar of epic proportions which our wedding set.

As I've said in the past, the Webster family loves to rejoice in the sheer joy of congregating people together in true celebration. I understand their love for gathering in festivity and I've always enjoyed every one of those events. Personally, I would be just as happy to have Dana and Ric be united in a small chapel of the Lord or even in our home, with the loving arm of Jesus wrapped around them. The true meaning of marriage can uniquely be reflected in these types of settings. Perhaps I'm just being selfish with giving up my daughter, but we tend to forget the real meaning behind this wonderful union. The devotion and promise of two people, who selflessly pledge their lives to one another, regardless of the challenges which come before them, surpasses any party like celebration in importance. Jesus will guide and rudder their hearts and remind them to never lose sight of their promise to each other.

Either way, I want to congratulate Dana and Ric on their engagement. They will make a fabulous couple. Both Dana and Ric are people of strong faith. I think Jesus is pleased that His two siblings listened to their hearts and chose to seek God's will together.

Age 56

California Verses

2003

A week or so ago I woke up amidst an odd sensation. In the mix was a slight level of urgency, nothing to alarming, but a feeling which seemed to be encouraging me in some way. Perhaps a better way to describe it was I felt a desire to try something I had never done, but overdue to attempt. I sat up to get a better handle on the feeling but after a few minutes the notion slipped away. I felt a bit disappointed that the urge had eluded me, but I had confidence the feeling would return at some point.

Today, my morning smile spread across my face even before my eyes opened. After prayers of thanks for a great overnight rest (courtesy of Jesus) the fleeting sensation from last week paid me a return visit. My eyes immediately opened in a wide-eyed glare, as though I was looking for clues as to what brought on my unusual but satisfying feeling. Rising from bed, I step into my slippers and make my way down the steps. Accompanying the pleasant feeling is a sense of creativity, compelling me to focus on some type of inspirational activity. My reception is strong, and this time I know I will get my arms around this elusive but motivating awareness.

It's Friday but I scheduled the day off. Kelly's last day of school was yesterday; she's off for the summer so I'm celebrating the day with her. Before she comes down, I decided to take my morning cup of caffeine into the family room to recline and further ponder my mysterious creative notions. Perhaps a relaxing stretch in the recliner will reveal answers to my elusive curiosity. With eye lids closed, and consciousness in full surrender, I'm out like a light. Before long I am again treated to the beautiful, lyrical words of our Lord...

Scribe your words
Not just in journal let thoughts be heard
Observe and write your hearts feelings
The moment will vanish in a vapor
Unless you capture the words paper

Pen your gift in prose and rhyme
Explain, expound let words expand
Express your visions on what you seek
From waters blue to mountains peak
And things which dwell from sea to sand

Evidently, Kelly has self- imposed a sleep in, and seems to be in no hurry to start her morning. Upon refilling my cup, I return to the family room and gladly apply uninterrupted focus to my just acquired inspiration. My previous thoughts first received last week, have now revealed a more defined direction. Over the years, I have been greatly gifted in the field of speech and the appreciation of language. Yet over fifty-six years of enjoying that blessing, after learning two foreign languages in high school, competing on the debate team, even expounding on editorial viewpoints over our University FM radio station, I have never formally written anything! Other than school assignments, I've never written a poem or a short story, let alone author a book. Amazingly, I've never written a paper on a specific topic, submitted a newspaper or magazine article, or wrote to my congressman. Other than my personal journaling, everything I've accomplished has been verbally spoken! Even when Brandon was in high school and shared the news of his writing contest, I was engrossed in thoughts of what I would write if I were in his position. But I didn't put a single word to paper, not even for fun. Finally, after all these years, Jesus clearly is suggesting I make a creative hard copy effort, encouraging me to see what the imagination produces. A satisfying smile of accord slowly forms on my face. A creative written effort is long overdue.

As the morning progressed, Kelly remained upstairs. With her shower completed over an hour ago, and our bedroom TV providing back ground noise, Kelly had been on an extended phone call. I figured it was work related, though it was a rather jovial call for school business. Likely she and another teacher were delighting in their newly received summer pardon from the rigors of education. Soon after the call was completed, she made her way down the steps.

"Guess who I was speaking to?" questioned my wife. Too early for riddles is my initial thought. "Jenny Masters", Kelly said with great glee, as she reclined back on a Lazy boy. Jenny of course is a dear college friend of ours, and a former dorm mate of Kelly's. Jenny was instrumental in getting Kelly an interview in the Cleveland area, allowing us to relocate back in 1970. Kelly began filling me in to the details of her morning call. Jenny and husband Ben are in the process of moving to California, to be close to their daughter Autumn. Her daughter attended university in CA. and has taken up residence in the Golden State. Autumn and Kevin recently had their first child. Jenny and Ben, now enjoying semi-retirement are moving to Whittier to be closer to their daughter and new grandchild. Jenny suggested a mini reunion / vacation is in order for the girls to catch up and share the blessing of their new addition. We actually had been considering taking some time off, before we got too close to Dana and Ric's fall wedding, so the timing of a California getaway is perfect. I know Kelly cannot wait to become a grandma someday, and hold her own grandchild. "Sounds good to me Kelly, go ahead and start looking at flights for us", I recommended. I guess I didn't have to tell her twice; she popped up from her chair, sprinted around the table, and then gave me a hug and kiss. As she bolted upstairs (vaulting two steps at a time) she announced she was going to call Jenny and then start travel arrangements. Wow, such excitement and energy; and she hasn't even had her morning coffee.

With Kelly literally off and running taking on travel duties, I recalled the last lines of my poem dream from earlier this morning...

From waters blue to mountains peak
And things which dwell from sea to sand

My initial thought was writing about the waters of the Atlantic, the Appalachian peaks, the Blue Ridge Mountains, and the sunny sandy beaches of the expansive Carolina coast. I mean this has been our home stomping grounds for over twenty years. No way would I have considered my writing topic to be 2,800 mile off target, on the other side of the lower forty-eight. We've never been to California; furthest west I've gotten was riding shotgun on the mighty Colorado, on our fabulous rafting trip when I was twelve. The thought of writing about the picturesque California coast with its rocky shore line, endless beaches, snowcapped peaks and desert sands is urging me to consider writing topics, even before we've booked our flights. One other thought has entered my mind; is the Lord encouraging me to write for personal satisfaction, or for a deeper purpose?

Today is travel day. We scheduled a late Monday afternoon flight, so with the time difference we should arrive for dinner local time. At this point we plan on flying back on Saturday, but our schedule is flexible. We want to allow plenty of time for Kelly and Jenny to catch up and I should have ample time to gain the mindset to start my inspirational writing efforts. I'm thinking I should have scenic, stunning writing topics in the geography alone, so I'm leaning toward developing a thought-provoking detailed writing style; at least that is my first impression. I'm going purely by instinct and open to any direction I feel inspirations lead me.

After arriving on the lovely west coast, and picking up our rental, Kelly phoned Jenny to let her know we safely landed and are ready to take on the California freeway system. During the call we learned Ben was called out of town. Ben is a retired structural steel engineer, but does consulting work. Jenny explained it is not unusual for him to be summoned on short notice to offer his expertise in the field when design issues come into play. I certainly will miss Ben's fellowship, but I'm excited about the opportunity to creatively write. With Ben away, it would also appear more time may have been opened up, to get the artistic juices flowing.

Upon our arrival, Jenny had a great dinner waiting for our travel weary bodies. Today was a day to celebrate good friends getting back together and catching up on life. Jenny and Ben have three adult children and this is grandchild number two, but the first girl. Seeing the glee and glory gleaming in Jenny's eyes is a wonderful blessing. It is also evident the emotion is heart tugging to Kelly; she hasn't stopped welling up since we've been here. I need to remember, these two are still the dearest of friends, sister like in many ways, and both possessors of two of the Lord's sweetest souls. Though distance has recently kept them apart, they were inseparable in college, and I suspect will be the same for the entire week.

Despite the great dinner and the interesting college stories (several of which I had not heard) the jet lag and time difference caught up to us. It may be 9:05 pm local time, but it's after midnight in our Carolina minds. After showers, prayers, and a quick journal entry, off go the lights. Amazingly, despite our long strenuous day, it is always difficult to turn off a racing mind, and wind down in a strange bed. I pray Jesus will soon relax me enough to bring this special day to a close.

Before too long I was in mid dream. It was dark and I could hear the pounding surf, though I didn't have a clear visual on the shore line. I sensed Kelly was nearby. Her mere presence creates a blissful tone as she greets the lonely waves coming ashore. The exhilaration pouring from her is consuming the entire area. With dawn breaking, I see her walking the shore, picking up shells and tucking them in a sack carried off to her side, supported by a strap slung over her shoulder. She picks up an occasional stone and heaves it in the surf as far as she could throw it. She is all smiles and her gleeful vibe engulfs me heart, soul, and spirit. Even in my dream she demonstrates the ability to absorb the bliss of the moment. This is what Jesus and I were thinking...

Her heart rejoices
A soul at peace
Her spirit soars
Above the roars
Of coastal voices
Pounding the surf
Never to cease

Do not look past
Her cheerful heart
To gather shells
As stones are cast
O'er water's edge
Into the swells

She moves with ease
On warm beach sand
Amid dawn's breeze
In spirit free
She turns and slows
To see you watching
As she goes

And there she stands
Calm and pleased
Since you are with her
To hold her hand
In moments seized

In the morning, I retained my thoughts of watching Kelly being herself, indulging in the jubilance of taking in the simple joys of nature. The peace I experienced while observing the caring unselfish heart which beats within her, is overwhelming in many ways. She is inspiring and encouraging and after thirty-four years of marriage, she (literally) is still the girl of my dreams.

After a quick morning shower, I descend down the stairs in search of a comfortable chair in Jenny's family room.   The girls are preparing breakfast and I am focusing my thoughts on writing.   Creative writing requires collaboration between the heart and the imagination.   Any subject, regardless of the writing topic can be expounded upon and presented in an inventive fashion to stimulate the reader.   The art of proper word choice and sentence structure to stimulate if not captivate the reader is all it takes.   Sounds simple... we'll see.

I then consider the myriad of writing subjects along the west coast, and recall what Jesus said in a dream a few weeks before our trip.   He suggested I put my thoughts down on paper before they vanish in a vapor. I agree, documenting thoughts in the emotion of the moment will best capture and reveal one's inner feelings.

By nature, I put emphasis on staying positive; to encourage and motivate people. I enjoy lending support to uplift them; whether they are down and out, or *living large in the Lord.* This is living life in the Lord; to go out and love one another as He asked us to do. While Jesus is perfect in every way, by ourselves we are far from that, but living in and through Him, we are as He is. By writing in a positive, impactful manner, I can perhaps capture His guiding thoughts and produce something inwardly rewarding and worthy of scribing. I think I am off to a good start at least I have a starting point. All I know is He is a positive motivator and one who will guide me in my new passion!

At breakfast, Kelly and Jenny finalized plans to visit Autumn, and her sweet newborn girl. We decided to take two cars. I will follow the girls to meet Autumn and her new arrival, and then head down the coast to seek my writing experiences.

I had a splendid visit at Autumn and husband Kevin's home. Both are very warm and welcoming, and baby Olivia is a precious little bundle. Once *Aunt* Kelly picked up the baby, prying Olivia from her hands was nearly impossible. I can only imagine the thoughts which must have been going through her *future gramma* mind. Before I left, we made plans to meet the girls for dinner on the coast, as I made my way back to Jenny's. While walking to the car, I decided to leave no writing topic is off the table. In part this is due to not knowing what I'd expect to encounter while out. My mind and my imagination were a clean sheet.

Now on the open coastal road, as the rocky shore line and sandy beaches came into view, the calm and peace I experienced in last night's dream swirled around the car as I motored south. I then slowed the car observing a small herd of sea lions, on a rocky cliff near a grassy beach. I found an area to pullover and safely park the car. I made my way down a hill and perched on a rock suitable for observing these magnificent local beasts. I quietly sat at a safe distance to view my aquatic friends enjoying their beachside accommodations. I closed my eyes in the serenity of the moment and took a deep breath of coastal air. Upon exhaling and opening my eyes, the number of sea lions had nearly tripled in the few minutes I had perched on the rock. They rest in groups, families perhaps all piled together sunning and barking at the sky and sea. The sea lion pups are celebrating a day at the beach and hop between rocks on the grassy beach head. I am in total isolation with the civilized world. Any coastal traffic is traveling in the overhead airways and inaudible from my position. It's Jesus, me, the sea lions and the beautiful California surf. With pencil in hand, I begin putting the inspiration of my visual surroundings onto paper …

Arriving in packs coming ashore
Brown furry spots dot the rocks they adore
The sea lions lie amid morning haze
To bask and rest on this sunny day

As pups flop and play in tall beachy grass
Their plan for today is to gather in mass
A reunion ashore after a day in the sea
To sun and recline and do as they please

They lay in contentment as I view from a distance
In each subtle movement at this very instance
They pause for a moment then turn my way
To see I am harmless and sharing their day

A day in which they play a large roll
Their mere presence brings joy to my soul
After a while on a whim they flee
Departing together they return to the sea

My poem was simply an attempt to capture a moment which brought peace and rest to my soul and jubilation to my entire being. I will share this tranquil segment of my life captured on paper with Kelly and Jenny, and log my poem in my journal. If I never write anything other than heart felt experiences like this one, I will be totally content with my writing efforts.

Without any notice, the playful giants took to the sea in a noise filled departure. I suspect their clatter was to alert the colony to assure no one was left behind. I also received their departure as a rousing good bye to me, as I bid my seafaring friends bon voyage from my rocky vantage point. I might even interpret a few barks as "bravo" for my attempt to capture their beach visit in writing. Why not? My mind and imagination are a clean sheet!

At some point I will be leaving this beautiful haven of God's handiwork, and head back to the car in search of a lunch worthy roadside eatery. Jesus and I are simply chillin' in the warm late morning California sun, viewing the last of the sea lions now going out of view. I have no clue as to what we will find around the next bend, but right now *We* are in no hurry to find out.

Age 57

Losing Dad and More

2004

Losing my dad last week was the most trying time I've ever endured. Regardless of our challenges, large or small, Jesus holds us tightly and accepts our pain, grief, worry and fear. His strength is ours, and that strength kept me whole during that painful week.

Despite Life's heart break, each day presents a new start. The Lord continues to shower us with daily gifts and many wonderful events. Dana and Ric were married in September of 2003, though we are still waiting to learn when we will be grandparents. This spring, Brandon sold his starter home and began building a new home somewhere in the burbs. Daryl and Sherry took a trip to the Middle East with their family of four. These are exciting family events, the best life can offer; wonderful blessings to behold, as we travel in fellowship with Jesus. This is how life goes; wonderful blessings of great elation, and sad days to weather, such as losing my dad this past week.   This is precisely why we should enjoy each moment to the fullest; since difficult times can quickly surface.

At eighty-three, Dad was in good health. His biggest difficulty was struggling with an arthritic left knee, which eventually required the use of a cane. Fortunately, his hands and arm remained strong so his dexterity was still reasonably good.

A couple of weeks ago Dad lost his balance while walking on some uneven concrete. While trying to stay upright he eventually fell backwards hitting his head. A neighbor witnessed the incident and immediately went over to assist Dad, while calling 911 as he neared him. Dad lost consciousness upon impact and despite the quick actions of the neighbor and the rapid arrival of first responders, Dad never recovered from the fall.   The good news for Dad; he was called home by the Lord and is now rejoicing in cheer with his parents and siblings. I miss him dearly, but happy for his reunion with those that left before him. I think what I will miss most about him is his ever-guiding hand and his trusty advice. His words seemed to be just what I needed at the time. How often have I said "Dad always makes things just right". That peace of mind and guidance I have enjoyed all my life is now gone.   I will miss our conversations, but there is rest in knowing I can lean on Jesus even more, now that Dad has passed.

It's been about three weeks since we bid Dad a tearful goodbye. The sting of our loss still looms today as it did, the day we found out we lost him. I am grateful God graced him with eighty-three glorious years. I had him for fifty-seven of those years; longer would have been great, but we will move forward with what life gives us. Right now, Mom is our main focus. Both Brandon and Dana love their gramma, and along with Kelly and me the four of us are keeping close tabs on Mom. We four, along with friends, are keeping Mom busy with daily visits. On weekends Mom stays over at our place. I think the Lord is keeping us focused on Mom as part of our coping mechanism. He is having us focus on what we have, rather than what we've lost.

In the weeks to follow, I let Jesus settle my heart. Fortunately getting a full night's sleep is again a reality. His rest is again mine, and His comforting words blanket me as we slumber waiting a new day...

Recall my son
Your father's grasp
The arms that held you
Whether first or last

His grip strong yet gentle
His love always shone
Whether you stood tall
Or felt alone

It mattered not
What you had done
If you were still
Or on the run

He stayed the same
If you lost or won
He never changed
You are his son

The next morning as I awoke, I realized my dream left me with a refocused perspective on my dad. I always knew him as our rock, one to rely on and one which our family could count on. I don't know if I ever verbalized exactly how much he demonstrated that trait every day of his life. Not just to me and Daryl as a loving parent, but to everyone who was fortunate enough to know him. He was unselfish with his time, generous to all, and willing to mentor. He was understanding and lived by the examples which he taught. As I now recall these are all the attributes people voiced of him, during his sixtieth birthday celebration. I listened to their words and recall nodding in agreement with their statements, but I don't think I appreciated those accolades as much as I do now. I hope he knew just how complete of a person he really was. Knowing how he traveled in the light of Jesus, I suspect he did. He wasn't the kind of person that needed to hear how wonderful he was. He simply lived fully and received every day as the gracious present that it is.

About a week after receiving my latest dream, things settled down and life got *normal* again. We were all adjusting to life post Dad, while visits and attention directed at Mom remained our focus. All of this changed when I received a phone call from my old high school friend and debate team partner Barton Lake.

Barton is a tax attorney in western Michigan, and one of the fabulous forty somethings that joined us on our reunion. We've only spoken a few times since, so when a call from an old friend comes in at 10:45 PM, one becomes rather guarded for bad news. Unfortunately, this call was one of those difficult messages to receive. Our old and dear friend Alex Snow perished in a small plane accident. Alex was in the sporting goods business and was on his way to Michigan for a sporting goods / sports memorabilia convention. As an experienced small craft pilot since his late twenties, Alex had logged hundreds of air hours in his thirty or so years of flying. During those years he had owned several planes. The plane that went down was a single engine job which he was in the process of selling. His buyer being in the same industry as Alex was also attending the convention in Michigan. The arrangement was to deliver the plane and meet the gentleman at a local airport. Unfortunately, about five miles outside the airport a sudden storm formed over Lake Michigan, taking Alex by surprise. The plane went down in near zero visibility conditions. Alex did not survive the crash landing which he attempted. I recently had spoken to Alex over the phone after Dad died; in fact, we chatted couple of times. That was typical of Alex … checking to see if I was doing okay. The loss however of my friend hit me like losing a twin brother. Alex was my first good friend. He was our high school star player, and possessed more humility than anyone I have ever known. He played for the love of sport and for the camaraderie of his mates. Alex was a gentleman and had an unrelenting yen for life. I am one thousand percent confident Jesus had His loving arms around Alex and held him tightly in his final moments.

After I completed my call with Barton, I sat there wondering what to do. It was Friday night and being empty nesters, Saturday wake up time for Kelly and I was at our discretion. She had a long week so I decided to let her sleep and not disturbing her with the sad news of our friend. I certainly could not go to sleep, so I opted for a glass of milk and a couple of brownies, then headed into the family room to click on the TV. It was time for a few late-night brainless comedy reruns, and my snack to help me absorb the loss of Alex. I actually settled on an old black and white detective movie; it must have been forty-five years old. I just needed some back ground diversion to help me cope with my aching heart.

This has been a very tough stretch. Just a short time ago we lost Dad. While we all struggled to let him go, we knew his life was a full one. He shared eighty-three glorious with family, friends, and acquaintances, before the Lord called him home in reunion. We will now be dealing with our current loss which is one of a far different variety. Alex was still young and energetic with much of his life ahead of him. He left behind a beautiful family that counted on him for support and nurturing. Alex was smart and caring, yet today his plane fell helplessly out of the sky like a rock tossed off a cliff. Here today and gone today, and he was my age! Fifty-seven years old, a beautiful wife, four children and many good years left in the tank. I've resisted asking the question "Why Jesus"? but the thought has entered my mind. I know everything happens for a reason, so I will remain patient on that front, and see what the Lord eventually discloses on this heartbreaking event.

Somewhere in my aching thoughts I dosed off and woke up about 1:45 AM. The black and white feature was over and I never found out who was behind the jewel heist. I decided to turn off the TV and head up to bed. My thoughts were with Karen, Alex's widow and their four kids, two of which are still teenagers and the other two in their twenties. His loss will leave a big hole in all of our lives, and a lot of prayer is needed to give everyone strength in his passing. It took a while but I finally fell asleep after some serious tossing and turning.

It was only a few weeks ago the gracious words of Jesus settled my heart when Dad passed away. Tonight, the Lord again called to me and gave me peace with the following reassurance...

Friends are special
Friends such as you
Friends are forever
Friends remain true

They'll never waver
In letting you live
Despite your behavior
They'll always forgive

They raise up your spirt
They set an example
Their trust is unquestioned
Their love more than ample

But of more importance
In all which they do
They cherish you dearly
They're thinking of you

The morning was peaceful and I could hear birds gently chirping on the patio. As I began waking up, I took a deep breath and found rest in the words which Jesus placed on my heart. The loss of a longtime friend should be richly celebrated for the good which he shared. Alex looked past my selfishness behavior, the day I met him in kindergarten. He exemplified the most courageous teamsmenship I've ever seen, after he went down with a devastating football injury. He appreciated my friendship after helplessly witnessing our team suffer a third straight loss, with him sidelined.   He then called my house to check on me and thank me, over my concern for him. He blessed my heart by accepting my groomsmen request when Kelly and I married.   The strong and wonderful memories of Alex go on and on. He will be greatly missed and he's left big shoes to fill, but his yen for life and his contagious spirit is what Jesus wants us to remember, when Alex comes to mind.

We will shed tears for a while. We will mourn and miss him, but we will get past the pain. But let tears of joy replace those being shed in sorrow. Alex was a positive and dedicated person, and a lover of life. He never grieved over his misfortunes and difficulties; I doubt he would want us to grieve too much over him now. May our tears be dried and the elation of all which Alex meant to us, be joyously celebrated!

Age 59

Red Zone Worries

2006

I just turned fifty-nine years old. Recently I've had conversations with my nursery owning, financial advising friend Dave Langley. Given retirement is only five or so years away, it's finally time to re-allocate all my investments, from any high-risk exposure. No more speculating down perilous avenues and watching the market go up and down like a yoyo. My only concern going forward is to be safely protected. I've diversified sensibly and have added some tangible investments, a property rental, and some undeveloped acreage. The market is strong, but perhaps too strong. My worry; what goes up must come down and the last thing I need at this point is an unexpected financial *surprise*.

Our lovely daughter Dana got married to Ric in 2003. Mostly through Kelly's doing, we had put funds aside for Dana's wedding. Dana had no idea Kelly was stashing away money for that event. As it turned out, the kids were already successful in business at the time of their engagement. When Ric and Dana found out Kelly was squirrelling away wedding funds, they both interceded and insisted we only pay minimal wedding costs. In turn, the kid's generosity enabled Kelly to feed her IRA an extra helping of peace of mind, for our collective retirement.

Financially, we are satisfied with the direction we have taken, and I am as protected as I can be for my retirement. By the way, retirement can't come soon enough. So why am I worrying? The usual; am I saving enough for retirement? Will I out live my money? Should I put more in physical investments, which provide a tangible presence, which I can sell or trade? Despite all the planning, one can easily go crazy overthinking and second guessing each decision. By the way, I absolutely love the career direction I took back in '82. Moving to the Carolinas and partnering with Dave Langley in the nursery and equipment sales business has been a total joy. Financially we did great, and the relationships we built in this loving area are priceless to our hearts. I simply want to enjoy the fruits of life and enjoy God's Green Earth while I still have a hearty body and a willing mind. I'm just a big fan of living in the elations of the Lord, and not so much a fan of working and earning, simply because I can. Just the same I tend to struggle in pulling the plug on the day to day work routine.

It's now mid-afternoon. I took the balance of the work day off. I had a working lunch with Dave Langley. My thoughts and concerns, for now at least, can again focus on a direction of my choosing. Sooner or later that route will lead to my investments and retirement plans. I know I should leave my worries in the hands of Jesus, but the flesh is rearing up and I just want to feel comfortable I will be able to properly support my family, as I always have done. Another words, its crunch time and I don't want to mismanage what we've been working toward, for all these decades. I know this is a control thing, but I'm finding it difficult to discover a comfort zone, in this retirement issue.

Now that I have arrived home, I see a note, which was left by Kelly on the kitchen island. She went to the market to pick up the needed items for tonight's dinner with the kids. She left a beautiful note, both sweetly and accurately written right on point. She knows me well; probably better than I know myself. She always manages to make sure all bases are covered. Listen to this...

Dan,

I've gone to the market to pick up some rib eyes (your favorite) as well as a coconut cream pie (your favorite)! I hope lunch with Dave Langley was pleasant; I'm sure he did his best to keep you calm and reassured. I suspect you may have been a "challenge" to his patience and expertise. Don't worry; we'll be fine in His (capital H) hands. Relax, take a nap.

Love, Kel

XOXOX

After all these years, she more than anyone can reel me in, calm me down, and make the world's problems vanish in an instant. In fact, I've settled down enough to take Kelly's suggestion; go out on the hammock and swing in the Lord's gentle breeze and take a snooze.

As I comfortably lay stretched out, I am smoothly swinging to and fro under the trees, and ready to nap in the late Carolina afternoon. I'm just about to nod off, as the restful words of Jesus fall gently upon my ear. Somehow, it seems like His message is a continuation of the words Kelly wrote on that brief note left on the table...

You have provided every day
All needs met for those you love
You've cared and gave in every way
And taught us well to rise above

Let no worry dissuade your cheer
Trust your faith will show the way
Allow no riches to feed your fear
As you calmly gently sway

My words for you speak to your soul
To harvest joy and afford you rest
Be assured you've made me whole
In you we have been truly blessed

Shortly after I awoke, I repeated those words in my head, probably six or eight times. Then I said the entire poem aloud. Immediately, after I softly spoke those verses, my eyes abruptly opened upon hearing Kelly gasp! Quickly I leaped out of the hammock, in an effort to see what may have caused her alarm. To my surprise, she was simply standing there. Her eyes were fixed on me as she stood with a package of steaks in one arm and a coconut cream pie in the other. There was a look of total amazement displayed on her face, and she was as motionless as a statue.

"Are you OK", I asked. "I think so", she unconvincingly replied. She took a deep breath, paused for a second and announced," start the grill Dan; I'll bring out the steaks in a sec". She quietly went into the house, put the pie in the fridge, then salt and peppered the rib eyes.

The seasoned steaks were resting at room temperature and the coals were beginning to ashen. Kelly looked up at me as I entered the kitchen. She gave me a pleasant smile and one of her beautiful patented winks. "You're in an interesting mood Kelly", I offered. "You had an interesting dream Dan", she countered. She went on to explain how she was thinking about me on the way home from the market. The words I uttered from my dream were Kelly's exact thoughts as she traveled back home, less the poetic phasing of course. "Heard from Jesus just now, I take it"? She asked. "I did" I replied. "He blessed me with a soothing assurance" I said. "But in my thoughts", Kelly accurately concluded.

We both just shook our heads; not in disagreement, but in awe of God's amazing love. Again we were treated to His gracious guiding words. We both marveled at His mighty way of sharing His love and His desire to enjoy life with us. He also reassured us our trusting relationship in each other, guided in His faithful provision, is stronger than any investment tip.

Dinner with the kids was great. The steaks were awesome and the pie disappeared, courtesy of Brandon and me both taking seconds. The best part of the evening was recalling the dream both Kelly and I evidently took part in. The eye contact and expressions Kelly and I shared (unbeknownst to the Kids) was priceless. The value of my entire portfolio does not even come close to the wealth of joy we both received, as we interacted in the poetic words of Jesus. Best of all, Kelly now knows firsthand (in a way at least) the blessings I feel when I am gifted through His touching verses. We are both deeply grateful He chose to verbalize through the thoughts and words of the most precious person in my life!

Fabulous days like this one are what life is all about. The family was together breaking bread, the meal was delicious, and the conversation centered on the thoughts, goals and dreams of my daughter and my son. We all agreed taking our life plans to Jesus, will lead us down the best paths. Best of all, in His graciousness, Jesus calmed and reassured me, by infusing the words of my beautiful wife, in His message. Between His strength and her adoring friendship and love, I have nothing to fear, while being wrapped in the arms of that amazing duo.

Age 61

Reflections of My Journey

2008

The world is a vast and complicated place. I try to comprehend the events that occur on our dear Earth with an open mind. Not in an effort to make sense of, or attempt to justify some of the things people do; let's pray we never get to the point of tolerating the awful things we do to one another. But we know we live in a fallen world. Scripture says trials, difficulties, and abominable acts are guaranteed. All we can do is stay vigilant, be prepared for these occurrences, and trust Him to get us through our tough times.

When tragedies arise, people are affected both directly and indirectly. Those on the *front line* of a heartbreaking event will be affected first. We as brethren to those befallen, then play an important role in aiding them, through love, prayer, and support. Jesus will guide us in lifting them up in the direction of His waiting and gracious arms. We become their encouragers, to seek His inspiration. He enables them to pour the weight of their pain and troubles on His eager and capable shoulders.

When I think of the times I and others came to the spiritual aid of a struggling friend, I think about the importance of reassuring them that they are loved. I realized what we do and what we say does make a difference in their healing process. We may never know the impact of our words until later, if at all. Regardless of that outcome, we come with a caring heart, to comfort them.

I had a friend who recently visited with an old neighbor of mine back in Ohio. My neighbor's name was Don Redmond. Don and I were not particularly close; more like acquaintances than anything. Don mentioned to my friend a conversation he and I had a few years back when I lived in that area. He recalled this quote from my grandfather, which I happened to share. "Honesty is the shortest road to a peaceful mind". He went on to say our conversation had turned to the topic of honesty, whereupon I shared one of Gramp's old sayings. I do recall sharing a number of his old adages, but I don't specifically recall that particular instance. Evidently, as my conversation continued with Don it seems he had been struggling with some truth issues. My shared quote then led him to *come clean* with his honesty issue. He went on to say he accepted his responsibility to be truthful, which brought relief to his heart and began mending a struggling relationship. What we say is important and the content of our words often have a profound impact on people. This goes for casual friends like Don or those who look to you as a significant part of their makeup. I had no idea my old neighbor was affected by that conversation. Who knows if anyone else may have received benefit from Gramp's wise words?

That evening I gave thanks for sharing the gracious influences of Jesus. There is no pride or boast in what took place; rather a feeling of peace that Jesus works through us when we live in His brightness.

As I retired the end of another wonderful day, overnight Jesus's words rang clear and cast magnificently in a dream...

Let hearts speak freely
Let truth be heard
Season speech wisely
Pick well each word

Speak not to hinder
But to aid and assist
Encourage each other
Leave no chance missed

May no lies be spoken
I'll temper what's said
Nourish your language
Through my daily bread

Let My preparation
Encourage your walk
Echo my goodness
Each time you talk

That morning at breakfast, I added a sprinkle of salt to my hash browns. The comparison of Jesus seasoning my words, as I salted my breakfast, left me in awe of our timely exchange. Salt and other seasonings enhance the taste of our food. Jesus will provide us with well-chosen words, allowing us to converse with flavor and civility, respect, and without judgment. In addition to that, as living messengers of His goodness, we are privileged the opportunity to further encourage and inspire one another in our challenging world. Planting His seeds of hope every day is fulfilling in many ways. Stepping confidently in His well guided direction assures a day bearing positive tones, sure to chime agreeably in our heart.

I shared the words of my dream with Kelly as we finished our breakfast. Her eyes lit up, as she hastily finished her last bite of toast, chased by a sip of juice. "I almost forgot, I had a conversation with Rita Schiller this past week", Kelly began. Rita is a teacher at Kelly's school. She is a bit younger than us; I'd say in her late forties. "She was telling me about her thirty-year high school reunion. She mentioned their twentieth reunion had rather unpleasant overtones. Many of the alumni were so focused on flaunting their successes, even to the point of boasting yearly salaries. The evening became tiresome and all the joy of getting together was overshadowed by the abundance of touting one's achievements, rather than old friends recalling their shared memories. Rita even skipped the twenty fifth reunion as a result of those conversations.   But determined to go to the thirtieth reunion, Rita borrowed one of your sayings Dan; in hope people would skip the bragging and simply fellowship in good spirit and conversation", Kelly said. This was my quote which she offered to her class...

Good advice – *check your ego at the door*.

Better advice – *leave it there once you leave*.

Many of her classmates took favorably to my quote and thanked her for posting it on the reunion website prior to the gathering. Evidently many of her classmates had also had enough of the boastful rhetoric, commonly displayed at the previous reunions. After the reunion, she told Kelly there was little to no conversation regarding financial standing or corporate ladder prowess. Instead, the conversation focused on family and children, and their recollection of the crazy antics and stories from their teen years.

"I'm so glad I shared your saying with Rita, Dan", Kelly recalled. "When Rita suggested she was going to skip the reunion, the quote jumped into my head and I sent it to her. That same day she posted it on the reunion website. I guess it had a huge impact", Kelly concluded.

Every once in a while, I run across a thought which I try to turn into a little saying. I'll bounce it off Kelly or the kids to see if there is any kind of positive reaction. If I get a pleasing response, I might try to glean it into the best phrasing. These are not meant to be earth shattering / profound life changing statements. But occasionally a few well-placed words speak good sense and culminate into good advice. Perhaps we might get the chance to share those words, if the appropriate situation asserts itself.

As we enjoy our years on Earth, we continually mature, certainly in body, but more importantly in mind and spirit. We learn, develop, grow, and flourish as brethren, sharing our experiences and nurturing each other to thrive in team effort, with the people God has put in our lives. In my heart, the greatest takeaway I have received from the bible is the Lord will accept us through our faith and trust in Him. Not by our deeds of accomplishment or triumphant successes, but by our desire to follow in trust. Our world, in all of its beauty and splendor, still sports an uneven playing field, influenced by our fallen nature. We as brethren can enter this world as rich and famous, be poor as dirt, or as common as the day is long. We can be born in majestic comfort, in war torn civil disorder, or a three bedroom one and a half bath bungalow... we don't get to choose. But somewhere in this myriad of possibilities, we do get to choose life through faith and prayer. As we seek guidance and direction in our lives, regardless of our environment, we will receive a spirited bearing on who we are. We'll also sense a faithful glimpse of what possibilities lay ahead. As we mature and our trust grows, direction becomes clear. That trust can begin as soon as we are ready to partner with the Lord.

As I mention in the past, my relationship with the Lord started at a very early age. Thankfully I longed for and trusted His guidance decades ago. In our connection, His comforting words of advice have cast light on one trail after another, uplifted me an incalculable number of times. Now at sixty-one I remain as grateful, if not more so than ever.

I read somewhere once you hit your sixties; you reach an important plateau in your life. Most sixty somethings still have a little spring left in the step, and are able to still do some of the things we enjoyed doing when we were younger. Most of us have gained enough wisdom to temper our expectations, and not endanger ourselves by doing those things we once did. Most importantly in our sixty plus years we have learned one very important valuable piece of wisdom; perspective!

How many times have we all heard the regretful refrain, *if I only knew then what I know now*? It is impractical to even think this way. Knowing what we know now is the culmination of knowledge gained by experiencing life. During my five plus decades of mortal participation, making observations, formulating decisions, and experiencing one life encounter after another, my maturity and resilience to life has taken shape. It is what I refer to as *the learning curve of life.* Our incurred wisdom, experience, maturity, and knowledge are what allow us to build perspective. For most of us, that is a lifelong process. Once we learn to get out of the way, (yes, we have a propensity to get in the way of ourselves, and hinder our own progress) and listen to the Lord and His guiding wisdom, we will step far more wisely.

I guess part of that hindrance is due to our own stubbornness and our insistence that we know what's best. As we get older and learn to increase our consultation time with Jesus, and begin to choose more wisely. Until then, we should humble ourselves a bit and realize we are not always aware of what is best for ourselves or others, but He is.

This is also the perfect time to repeat what I said a few years back. Something which helped Kelly's teacher friend Rita Schiller when shared with her class reunion group...

Good advice – *check your ego at the door*.

Better advice – *leave it there once you leave*.

That balance of humility in oneself and trust in the Lord, at least in my case, has proven to be a path always worthy of traveling.

Age 63

Mom Webster's Last Retreat

2010

Springtime in beautiful upstate South Carolina offers ravishing views and mind easing settings. Areas near the mountains enjoy comfortable temperatures, as brooks and streams naturally fed from the Appalachian create tranquil waterscapes. Nestled in this inviting scene is beautiful Angel Mission Resort. Her expansive acres reach across rolling hills and along relaxing creeks. This breath-taking hideaway is well known for hosting church and family retreats, business getaways or simply soul relaxing vacations.

The village features three separate units, each tastefully situated to provide ample seclusion from its counterparts. The waiting list for any of these prized villas is nearly two years. This coming mid-May weekend, the Webster clan is slated to descend on one of these units for a three-day reunion/retreat. Attending will be our four and Dana's hubby Ric, Ron, Susie and their girls, many of Kelly's aunts, uncles, and cousins, and of course Mon and Dad Webster. Our clan will unite in the famous 4 Fs of Webster family acclaim; family, fellowship, food, and festivities. We will also engage in the 4 Rs of soothing bliss; reunion, retreat, relaxation, and reflection. Ron and Susie came up with that combo of Rs to capture our intentions for the retreat. Somewhere secluded in the all of those words lays the name for our gathering. Kelly and me will take on the task of naming this blessed event, and create a sign to hang on our villa entrance.

Amassing in large numbers with family is always a special occasion. This particular gathering will feature some significant overtones. Mom Webster is eighty-five and Dad is eighty-seven. Mom has fought off a few issues which come with the territory of life in the eighties. Dad walks with a cane to steady his aching hip and knee. "Too much golf over the years", as he puts it, "but the memories of sinking a forty-foot birdie is a price I'll gladly pay". I've always admired his attitude toward life, and his dedication to *stay the course*. Dad Webster, you are every man's example. Despite these all too familiar characteristics of aging, Kelly and I otherwise have two bright, witty, loving parents in our dear Mom and Dad.   Given those noted age related facts, the family wants Mom and Dad to enjoy all of us together, while all of us are still able.

With preparations finalized and all plans in place, retreat arrival day is upon us. Two years in the making and the Lord has apprised us a beautiful weekend, with the promise of mid seventy-degree temperatures and zero chance of rain, right through Monday... the perfect forecast! What a blessing to start our reunion/retreat on such a fantastic note; a note however, which will sound in a far more alarming tone, before too long.

As Kelly and I pack up the SUV, I pleasingly look at the sign Dana and Ric printed at AGF... it reads;

Webster Family Reunion
Partaking in the 4 F's
(Family Friends Food Festivities)
Awakening in the 4 R's
(Reunion Retreat Relaxation Reflection)

The last of our bags has been loaded in our vehicle, and it is crammed to the brim. In typical Lowe/Webster fashion, we again managed to pack a months' worth of stuff for a three-day weekend. In my defense fishing gear and guitar cases take up quite a bit of room. We've barely left enough room for Brandon. He'd typically either take his own car or piles in with Ric and Dana, but my dear daughter and son- in-law graciously offered to chauffer Mom and Dad to the retreat. They flew in from Toledo the night before and stayed at Dana's place.

Its noon Friday and we've just arrived. Kelly and I along with her Aunt Carla and Uncle Bob comprise the set up contingent. We're busy getting room accommodations from the desk, and getting things set up in the main meeting area. An informal lunch buffet will be available during the afternoon. The Lodge staff is preparing a wonderful buffet style dinner which will be served at 6:30 PM.

One of the first decisions we made during our pre retreat meetings was to have our host facility provide meals. This would avert *certain* family members, from spending too much time in the kitchen area slaving away in prepping, serving, and clean up duties. These tasks have a tendency to linger from one meal to the next. All of us are here to enjoy a family retreat and reunion, not pull K-P duty. For Friday night dinner, we picked a wild game entrée. Roast pheasant, turkey, and duck, all locally and freshly harvested. After all, this is a Webster family gather, why miss an opportunity to indulge in a savory meat trio?

By 3:30pm everyone had arrived and was enjoying food, hugs and cheer in the main meeting hall. Kelly, Ron, and I were splitting time visiting and setting up our guitars and equipment in the corner, preparing for a night of music and laughs. We'll have Ron, Dana and me on guitar, Uncle Bob on bass, and Brandon on Drums. Once my daughter got her guitar form Epps Music back in 1985, Brandon did get drums a few months later. My goodness, that was twenty-five years ago; where did the time go? By the way we still regularly see the Epps guys if you'd been wondering. We've had them over for barbeques and to jam several times, since the reunion of forty somethings. We've also spent many wonderful afternoons on Melvin's boat, just chillin'. Great guys; love 'em both.

As evenings go, this was an off the chart ten! My first ever taste of pheasant did not disappoint; the staff served up endless trays of food and desserts in stealth like fashion. The only time I noticed any of them was when peach pie, topped with peach swirl ice cream was announced. The pies were fresh baked in Angel Mission ovens, and the ice cream was churned in their dairy. "This is a dessert from heaven', claimed Uncle Bob, after he took his first bite. Hard to argue with that, with chocolate syrup on top, perfect! By shortly after 11:00 pm, the band had dwindled from our starting six (plus walk up vocalists as the urge struck) to Ron quietly playing and singing an acoustic Beatles set, as songs came to mind. If there is a guitar in the room, Ron will be on it nonstop, until we turn the lights out on him.

With the last of the Webster faithful exchanging final goodnight hugs closing a glorious day, Kelly, Ron, Susie and I quietly stand in a small circle. We share our favorite moments from our first day; then close in pray, one at a time with me as the last to speak…

Father, we are thankful and grateful You safely brought us together; to share our hearts and love for each other. The peace You draped over our family has given us an evening we will never forget. Our endless love for You, is our thank you for Your daily gift of each new day. Bless and watch over us tonight, keep us safe and bound in your arms, so we can all share a new day in your light. In your name, Amen!

Nearly exhausted from one of the best days ever, I think Kelly and I could have fallen asleep the moment we hit the sheets. As I walked toward the bed, I was determined to stay awake long enough to capture the day's incredible events. But for the first time I can ever recall, I fell asleep in mid entry, with open journal draped across my chest. My partially submitted thoughts began to describe the level of excitement, which was created the second the first Webster group arrived. Before long my totally drained body succumbed to the inevitable comfort of the king-sized bed Kelly and I were sharing. While rejoicing in dreamville, Jesus offered His loving and revealing words to complete my entry…

How precious are we
Amassing together
Supportive and caring
Now and forever

Our passions have brought us
From near and far
To laugh and break bread
And embrace who we are

Tomorrow I'll shepherd
Your blessed assemblage
Which promises moments
To love and encourage

While watching my flock
I'll safely hold her
My arms will console
As worries occur

I awaken with a bit of a cautious smile. My smile travels from ear to ear and why not, we are amidst a blessed assemblage, as Jesus put it. But He also closed on a bit of a guarded note. It appears one of our ladies will experience an alarming episode of some concern. Within seconds of digesting that realization, Dana entered our room; "Mom, Dad, its Gramma, something's wrong", my girl said with great concern. It didn't take long for my unsettled thoughts to be realized. I quickly woke Kelly and dashed over to look in on Mom.

After ten or fifteen minutes of careful observation, Mom began to perk up a bit and insisted she was alright. This was a positive sign to see, but just a few short minutes ago she was light headed and somewhat disoriented. Dana said Mom told her she wasn't sure where she was upon awaking. Granted this is a strange setting for all of us, but the light headedness is still a concern. Several more minutes passed and Mom seemed like her normal self. We decided the long day and a flight the afternoon before were likely contributors to Mom's rocky start this morning. Several of us discreetly agreed to keep a very close eye on her, and at no time will she be without someone observing her for even the slightest alarming symptom. We know Jesus has His arms around her and is keeping her safe.

Breakfast was now being served featuring scrambled eggs and waffles, and just about every possible breakfast side known to man. Once we took to the outdoors, we were treated with a generous list of activities ranging from fishing and paddle boating to biking, trail walking, or simply relaxing in one of the pavilions for chat and reflection. Both lunch and dinner were scheduled to be served outdoors and shared together in traditional Webster fashion.

Day two was far less stressful for Mom and every one of us spent quality time with her. We all engaged in delightful conversation and I learned a few secrets about

Kelly that I never knew. When she was seven, she wanted to be the first female firefighter in Toledo history! That didn't happen of course, but even then, she had a servant heart and wanted to dedicate her life to helping or enriching the lives of others.

Day two ended on an amazing note. After dinner, we returned indoors and shared in beautiful harmony as our musicians led us in heart inspiring praise worship. We sang everything from old gospel standards to the most current worship releases. Everyone left the room and headed to bed humming or singing one tune or another. As we closed our near perfect day, all of us were greatly relieved Mom experienced no further incidents of concern.

Come Sunday morning after a peach and berry covered stack of pancakes, we went into the main area and began an impromptu Webster style church service. Uncle Bob shared a short inspirational story on the joys of sharing, and living life with a giving heart. We again played and sang praise song and picked up where we left off last night as though we'd never stopped. I closed the service in prayer, asking Jesus to extend travel mercies to all of us, as we readied to depart after lunch. We also asked Him to keep his arms gently and safely secured around Mom, so she could continue to be incident free while gaining back her strength.

The Lord protected all of us and safely returned us home. Everyone said this was the best reunion/ retreat ever. Mom and Dad spent a relaxing day with Dana and Ric, and comfortably flew home to again be under the watchful eye of Ron and Susie back in Toledo.

Two weeks have passed since our retreat and everything seems to be back to normal (whatever that is). Kelly retired from teaching last year after forty glorious and rewarding years. She spread the word she had decided to do some private tutoring at our home. She was just about to return a couple of calls from students who had left word they were interested in receiving her tutoring, when our phone rang. On the other end of the line was Ron, calling to let us know Mom was taken to the emergency room. She again was light headed and felt faint and actually fell while in the kitchen. Dad called EMS and then called Ron, who arrived at their home just in time to see Mom put in the back of the vehicle. Ron followed the emergency team to the hospital where she was taken for treatment. Early indications revealed Mom suffered a stroke.

The next hour or so was nothing short of total chaos. I was busy bathing our new corgi Neil, who managed to find and slip into a mud puddle somewhere on the side of our home. Neil was barking and tussling amid the cleanup attention I was trying to administer. Kelly was on the phone scrambling to book the next flight from Charlotte to Toledo, amidst the noise and clatter Neil and I were creating. As we attend to our two tasks, our thoughts were on Mom, while thinking about Dad and what he must be going through. Ron indicated the stroke seemed to be a serious one.

That afternoon the noise and disorder from earlier today was exchanged for the uneasy silence of waiting for word on Kelly's mom. By 8:15 pm Kelly's flight finally landed. Ron picked her up and the two of them made a beeline to the hospital. I was stretched out in the recliner with my cell gripped tightly in my hand waiting for her call. I observe Neil laying on his back, freshly bathed and blown dry, stretched out with all fours straight up in the air, without a worry in the world. I asked Jesus to ease my worries and offer me some of the peace Neil is experiencing, as I anxiously waited for Kelly's update.

Sometime around 11:20 pm the house phone rang, indicating Kelly's cell number on the caller ID. I took a quick breath and answered the phone with optimism, though I had been preparing for the worst. A slightly shaken but still composed Kelly Lynn began sharing a detailed description of her Mom's condition. The incident Mom endured while at the reunion was actually a mini stroke. The one she suffered today was a bit more debilitating. Her speech is slowed but not slurred.

179

She seemed to have all facial movement but she did not have much movement on her left side. When Kelly left, she was still in ICU. "The next seventy-two hours are very critical Dan", Kelly stated with noticeable concern. "I'm worried, but at least she's in the best of care', she said with confidence. "I know Kel, the hospital is one of the best around for these types of emergencies", I said in an attempt to comfort my worried wife. "Yes, I know Dan, but I'm not referring to the staff of specialists at the hospital; certainly, they are outstanding professionals, and we are grateful to have them care for Mom. I'm referring to our gracious Lord". I paused for a second; leaving the line free of conversation, amazed by the poise and faith of my trusting wife. She just experienced perhaps her longest and possibly most trying day of her life. She jumped through hoops and due to weather conditions and mechanical issues; she was forced to endure a ten-hour zig zag, plane changing flight plan. The entire time, Kelly had to hold things together, while no doubt wondering if her Mom was still with us. She did all this simply to hold the hand of her Mom, as she helplessly lay in a post-op bed.

"Mom was sedated and pretty much out of it, but at one point she opened her eyes and turned her head toward me and smiled. She then closed her eyes and went back to sleep", Kelly said. "It was nice she knew you were there Kel", I consoled. "Her look and smile were just what my aching heart needed, Dan. That difficult moment was suddenly covered in calmness. The room got still and I managed to find joy in the moment, and I claimed it", my girl said with renewed vigor. "I then whispered in her ear; *I love you Mom.* She managed to return a small smile. At that point I felt comfortable enough to leave".

Fortunately, her long and trying day ended on an optimistic note. Kelly left the hospital and spent the night with her dad at his house. Her return plans will be dictated by Mom's condition. My plans are to retire the day, journal, and try to get a good night's sleep. This may be easier said than done; this marks the first time in quite a while that I will be retiring the day by myself. It's a little lonely with the left side of the bed vacated. I think Neil sensed my troubled soul, given Kelly is away. He vacated his little bed in the corner and jumped up on our bed, positioning himself in the area where Kelly's feet would be. Neil's kind efforts eased my mind enough to finally fall to sleep. Jesus too graciously extended that feeling of harmony that He placed over the ICU. I confidently corralled Christ's calm contentment in complete composure. (I needed to do that).

Soon His words summed up today's events and those days going forward, as I rested in His peace...

Her kind, caring soul
Gives without thought
I'll keep her whole
To fulfill all she sought

No pleasure is greater
For her to explore
Then sharing each moment
With those she adores

She's strong when we're weary
Consoles when we worry
She eases our pace
When our heart tends to hurry

For all she has done
We remain grateful
But time has escaped her
To be steady and able

Her elations are endless
Her life we've been gifted
More joy will be claimed
Once her pain is lifted

As morning broke, the only audible sound I could detect was our pup Neil, humming as he exhaled. He was still asleep though his head was hanging off the edge of the bed. How dogs can get comfort in sleeping in that position perplexes me. Just the thought of blood rushing to my head makes me nauseous. As I prop up in bed my movement wakes Neil prompting him to snuggle up by my side. I begin thinking about the exchange Jesus shared with me overnight, and remain positive about my thoughts on Kelly and her mom. Without question my dream captured Mom's servant heart and her devoted love she has for all of us. Mom Webster is one of the most adoring creations ever to draw a breath on God's Green Earth. I give thanks for her and the lovely daughter she raised and guided.

After a few days in the hospital Mom gained enough strength to begin speaking slowly and quietly. She was transferred to another room and soon would begin in-house treatment and therapy to strength her stroke ravaged body. Kelly then felt comfortable enough to schedule her return flight home.

A day or so after Kelly returned home, I shared the words Jesus spoke to me while she was still in Toledo. "He's not quite done with her yet", I said. He said He'll sustain and keep Mom in the life she sought. Kelly looked at me with a smile and a look of caution. "What's wrong Kel", I curiously asked. Kelly replied, "Before I left, I asked Mom if she felt OK. I told her I'd stay all summer if she needed me. Do you know what she said, Dan"? Kelly asked.   I quietly shook my head in anticipation of her response. "She asked me if there was anything I needed", Kelly said with her voice bound up in emotion. "Can you imagine; Mom is lying in bed, almost as helpless as a newborn, and she was asking me if I was Ok or needed anything at all", Kelly said in awe of her

Mom. "What did you say"? I asked Kelly. "I simply did what I always do, I whispered in her ear *I love you Mom*, and I quietly left to look in on Dad at their house", my grateful wife explained.

A few weeks later Mom was still in the care of the hospital and was working on small strengthening exercises. She was showing improvement, though concerning developments were beginning to surface. Soon complications decreased her ability to improve and we slowly began losing her. That evening Kelly took the call from Ron that Mom could no longer hold on and Jesus called her home. After hanging up the phone in the kitchen, she quietly walked into the family room and curled up on the recliner. My first inclination was to follow her and give her a reassuring hug, but something told me to give her a few minutes to begin absorbing what she just learned. Just about the time I started to head over to her she quietly asked me to get my journal, and bring it into the family room. I was slightly surprised by the timing of her request, but I obliged and handed her my journal before sitting down on the sectional next to her.

Before she opened the journal, she asked if she could read aloud the words Jesus laid on my heart while she was with Mom in the ICU. I nodded yes and she easily found the entry highlighted in blue. Kelly read the poem to me, and then looked at me with a satisfied and resigned expression.   "Dan, this poem about Mom perfectly describes her entire life, and her feelings for us. Her blessings came by giving and her happiness came from fulfilling the needs of others. I think she was able to leave us knowing we would miss her, but aware that we'll be OK in letting her go. She was ready for Jesus to lift her pain and elate in the joy of eternity", Kelly concluded as she gently closed my journal on her lap. For a few minutes we sat in reflection of our personal thoughts. Clearly Kelly is still thinking about her mom's servant giving heart, and hasn't even begun to deal with the grieving process.

In the hours and days to come, Kelly will soon begin grieving mightily over her loss. Tears will spill and emotions will be torn in multiple directions, but let's hope her tears will flow in the joy of knowing Mom is walking in the garden with the Lord, after living a long, fulfilling and giving life.

Age 65

Finally, Retirement!

2011

When I retire it will be for good. This is a concise statement; it is simple and straight forth. However, two key principals must be in place to make the decision to retire a successful one. First, are you comfortable in your financial position; whatever that may be? Second, and possibly more important, are you physiologically ready to retire? In other words, do you possess a willingness to say good-bye to your day to day business world existence? When stated in that light, it's no wonder many people resist even the notion of retirement.

The impact of voluntarily walking away from what you have done for your entire life, i.e. working for a living, is a huge step. Whether you were employed by a number of different companies, or you were "old school" like yours truly and basically stayed in one industry, retirement to some seems like the beginning of the end. It's the last destination on a cross country train ride, the last slice of pizza in the box, the last ornament to be hung on the Christmas tree. Yep! It's all downhill from here, the party's over! WRONG! This is what you have been working toward; this is what you have earned! You now have the ability to do what you only had time to do on the weekends. As I like to put it, "do all the things which work got in the way of". Pardon my ending that last sentence on a preposition, but I stated that wonderful point, in that manner for a reason. This was simply the best way to say that you shouldn't work your entire able-bodied life away. Save your money sure, invest by all means, diversify and prepare for your golden years, absolutely, but never work solely for the purpose of proving you can still do it. *Golden years;* please join me in disliking this annoying term. It suggests the only necessary shopping you have left is touring the showroom floor at the funeral Home, in search of your pinewood overcoat. Look, your body has fewer years left than you have already lived, I get that; but your brain still thinks like it is twenty-five or thirty. I'm simply saying make sure your body still has some useful miles left on the odometer.

Let me share with you a strong argument for "quitting while you are ahead". This is the term I use for retiring while you still have a willing and able body and a keen mind. I've known several people who worked well into their seventies, only to find out; (practically overnight in some cases) they simply can no longer effectively perform. As with a punch-drunk boxer looking for that final payday, the skills are diminished and retirement is a remittance long past due. The problem now becomes even further muddied. You passed up your chance to retire gracefully; now you have backed yourself into the proverbial corner and you must retire. Even worse, learning you may be forced to retire, and not leaving on your terms!

This is where too many of us get it all wrong. Retirement should be enjoyed as a freedom, a breaking of the shackles as it were, and a liberation from "The Man". A friend once told me; "if the announcement of your retirement was not met with a bit of surprise from coworkers and even a touch of panic from management, then you waited too long".

In my case, I started in earnest to plan for retirement in my late forties. Frankly, I never dreaded the day when I would no longer be working full time. My biggest concern wasn't aging, but not being in a proper position to gracefully age. I adopted this acceptance of retirement in my later forties for two distinct reasons. This was about the time I was learning how the wonders of science were advancing in areas, allowing us to live far longer than any time in human history. Living to be one hundred years old or related to someone who will hit that milestone, will be common place. I also read a man in his sixties reaches the most satisfying and rewarding time in his life. He typically is still young enough to do many of the things which he enjoyed earlier in adulthood. He also has seen or experienced much of what life has to offer. In turn he has become wise, tolerant, knowledgeable, savvy, and likely developed a mature and well-versed feel for what life is all about. Why in the world would someone want to be tied to the office, and not enjoy those wonderful abilities on your own terms?

When I hit sixty-four, I was already in a full retirement mindset. I was in my last full year of work; only Dave Langley and Travis Betts were aware of my intentions. My problem wasn't keeping up, or excited to share (gloat) the fact that this was going to be my last full year. My problem was struggling to keep focused and stay determined to give my all to the company, which had been my financial provider. As that year went on, I had prayed every night for the Lord's guiding words. I asked for strength, to keep me focused and to maintain a positive work ethic. For weeks I asked for His direction and heard nothing. I began to wonder if I was really ready to retire. Perhaps I was asking amiss, or maybe I just wasn't intently hearing God's word.

Exhausted and somewhat exasperated by the issue, one evening, I decided to leave my retirement issue off my prayer docket. Instead, I prayed for strength for my struggling friends, good fortune to continue to grace the Nursery in my retirement, and a number of other concerns, which were weighing on my heart. Wouldn't you know it! That very night I received Jesus's peace laden words. Oh how He can settle my being in an instant! This was what He shared...

No task is routine if the mind is embattled
The heart is convinced the field 's not level
From surface to core, you've become rattled
As corporate longings no longer revel

My son you savored your great times
Yet knew each trial still bared a meaning
But joy is waning and no longer chimes
And all which gave promise, has little feeling

I will forever provide the way
My hand on your shoulder sharing My will
Follow My voice, you'll never stray
I'll calm your heart, and keep you still

Your needs will be met; true and fulfilling
Provisions abundant; never to cease
My miracles many, exciting and thrilling
Can fill every moment giving you peace

Wow, deep sigh! I knew now, this was the time to enlist all my veteran experience, amassed and groomed over the decades, and confidently announce my retirement plans for my next phase of life. To you I say enjoy your hobbies and passions, travel, play music, read, write, do crafts or garden, live and enjoy life as your desires call. Whether your joy is in volunteer work, or surrounding yourself with family or beloved friends, simply live and love life in God's direction, as He leads you. You have earned it!

Can I still perform my job tasks? Yes, I'm certain I can. But I'm ready to hand the reins over to the next willing and able person, with the passion to fill the position as it should be filled; with desire and verve and a hunger to give it your all!

Experience life, make sacrifices along the way as your heart directs you, but trust and ask the Lord to continue to be your provider. Let Him be your strength. Allow Him to attend to your trusting heart. He will guide you well, as always.

Age 66

Life for a Future Grampa

2013

I have been retired for a year and a half. In that duration of time, I've managed to avoid the compulsion which plagues many retirees; succumbing to the urge to go back to work. I've returned to the nursery several times to visit my working buds, and to see how the place is progressing in further establishing its foot print in the industry. As for missing the day to day; nope... I'm perfectly happy I'm retired.

Mind you, I'm not against seniors taking on a part time job, for a couple of days a week. Something simple or fun would be nice. Besides, a few extra "mad money" dollars would fit nicely in any senior's pocket. A job similar to the first job you experienced as a teenager would be a good example. Bagging groceries at Mel's Market, was my first job. I loved it there; it was before the days of asking the monotonous question; paper *or plastic*? In those days, everyone got a good sturdy paper bag. If the shopper walked to the store, or the items were bulky, we double bagged for safety. This is the type of job I want if I were to decide to return to the ranks of the employed. No stress and little aggravation. I want simple questions, which can be easily answered. Something along the lines of, chocolate or vanilla, debt or credit, is as far as I'm willing to go. I see no reason to invite any more complexity into my life. After all, I'm retired and enjoying life!

To be sure, there may be situations whereupon a person may need to go back to work. A financial emergency or a family situation could dictate returning to the needs of a weekly paycheck. I am referring to going back to work *voluntarily*, due to boredom, or simply having too much time on your hands. If that is the case, clearly a retirement plan was not properly implemented. Possibly there was still too much of a desire to work and earn? In my case I had no doubt I was ready. Financially I had been preparing, and starting to count down the months and days. I also felt the roaring flame to produce and prosper for the company, was quickly reducing to a flicker and about to go out like the pilot light in an old hot water heater. Clearly, I was ready to move on to the next phase of my blessed mortality.

So, the gold watch I was given at my retirement dinner has spent the majority of its time in my sock drawer. It is as retired as I am. Since then I've been enjoying the second segment of life; what I call active retirement. Sure, the hips are a bit achy in the morning and I no longer can eat like a teenager. Then again nobody should eat like a teenager, not even a teenager. Speaking of eating, the first thing I did once I retired was instill a few more diet restriction on our eating habits. As much as I knew exercise would be even more important, I figured I'd likely become less active. Desserts were further limited and I cut out most bread carbs; I not only lost a couple of pounds, but I have more energy. That boost in energy is what I will take into my next phase of life and I will need it. This past week I receive the most blessed news I could possibly receive. After two years of retirement, Daniel Ethan Lowe, retiree, will soon be Grampa Dan. I heard the fantastic news from Kelly, that Dana and Ric are expecting a child sometime in October. I am elated beyond words and Kelly is totally beside herself. She's laughing, crying tears of joy, fist pumping, high fiving, and leaping up and down with unharnessed emotion. Her cell phone is getting a work out as well, given she is calling just about everyone she knows, to share the news of this wonderful gift from God.

As the evening went on, Kelly should have been slowing down, but the adrenalin was still pumping in overdrive. Her cell phone was nearly dead and unable to keep up with her breakneck pace. As she finished up her call, in preparation to go to her next, she reached for her phone charger. I gently intercepted her hand in an effort to divert her intention. As she completed her call, I suggested it be her last for the evening. She agreed, though she was still beaming like a light house. I finally convinced her to try to wind down and get ready for bed.

I was pleasantly relaxed and giving thanks to Jesus for the wonderful blessing Dana and Ric were given. I also ask the Lord to gently peel Kelly off the ceiling, and quietly calm her enough to get ready for bed and go to sleep. It seems like Kelly is getting her second wind, perhaps her third, either way it is clear she is far from being ready to turn in. I decided to dim the lights and pop in a CD, which plays relaxing and calming sounds. I settled on the track which offered pounding surf on a soothing deserted beach. After about five minutes, Kelly exhaled in a big sigh, rolled over and with a sweet smile still proudly displayed on her face; she slowly dropped off to sleep.

As I gave thanks for the day's events, I thought about the excitement we shared today. News of a new baby assures we will be receiving a variety of new joys and experiences. I think back at how things have changed since the days when our generation brought new lives into the world. Dana is an example of many of those changes. First, she is thirty-nine and like many parents in her generation, she and Ric prioritized to establish a career and worked with diligence to prepare for their family. I think Kelly and I would have enjoyed being grandparents a bit sooner, but that was not for us to choose. Speaking of choosing, Dana and Ric decided to learn if they were going to be blessed with a boy or a girl. It turns out The Good Lord will be gracing them with a little girl. Also, Dana wanted to be a stay at home mom, so she positioned herself to work until she was ready to take motherhood on full time. She wanted to raise her child her way; in her words "if this child turns out to be a mess, that's one me". That's my girl, always taking on responsibility like a bulldog. She has the beauty and heart of her mom and independence and drive of her dad. God love her!

It's late and Kelly is asleep; I'm ready to retire as well. I give thanks to Jesus for the wonderful gift of a new addition to arrive later in the fall, and ask that He protect His new little sister, as she prepares to join the world. With prayers said, I'm prepped to doze off with a smile on my face.

A short time later I awoke, not certain if I was dreaming, given the news of our expecting a new addition to the family. In the quiet of the overnight I distinctly heard the cooing and giggle of a new born child. As I became aware of this happening, I listened more intently, but the tiny voice quieted back into the silence of the night. I wondered if this was a dream or my vivid imagination playing tricks on me, by previewing the sounds and sensations of things to come. Either way, I was pleasantly touched by the notion of this glorious little interlude piercing the overnight hush. I am certain the Good Lord in some way had His hand in that lovely exchange.

A short time later, once I did finally fall into a comforting sleep, I heard Him call as He has done some many times before...

Put no expectation on future days
Enjoy each moment in Father's time
Our book of souls awaits their phase
To enter life at the moment sublime

Soon she'll shine in her debut
May brightness beam as she goes
Her loving soul and spirit true
Will glide in grace as rivers flow

She'll possess awareness
Her heart beats attuned
To things which surround her
As she blossoms and blooms

Her precious voice was but a taste
Of lovely words she soon will speak
Love and teach and never waste
The moments she and you shall seek

Well there you go, thank you Jesus! What a wonderful message and the fourth verse I believe confirmed what I heard was a sample of the blessings our family soon will experience. Deep within my being I felt this little soul and spirit, reach out to me, as she is forming in the nurturing womb of my daughter. She is already teeming with life and eager to seek the freedom of beginning her mortal existence. I can only imagine my elation, once she is born. Dana is a near clone of Kelly in every way, and now there will be a third generation of this marvelous lineage. I can't wait for that day to come.

For those who long to see a miracle performed by God, look no further than the people who you share your life. Each of us as a miracle, created in the highest design for a distinct purpose. All of us are special in His chosen way. While there are times when the purpose of His will is difficult to understand, eventually we will comprehend the reason behind those experiences. The book of Life needs no editing; God's Will was flawlessly created. Praise our creator for His perfection.

Age 67

Our Forty Fifth Anniversary

2014

-The Beach Front Celebration-

Earlier this spring, Kelly and I fondly chatted about our eventual fiftieth wedding anniversary (God willing) in 2019. We determined a celebration of our forty fifth, while still in our sixties, could prove to be more exciting, than reveling at seventy-two.

I've mentioned how Kelly and I have always made an honest effort to stay active and remain *reasonably* physically fit. Kelly remains quite fit; it's me who reduces our collective condition, but I'm actually in the gym again and feeling optimistic. We're also long overdue for a nice vacation. We decided to celebrate our near half century anniversary over an entire week; three days on the Atlantic coast (celebrated with our Carolina family) then three days in Ohio (with our Toledo area contingent) to wrap a week of rejoice and fellowship.

A friend of Dave Langley has a beach house in Charleston, SC. The place is a lovely two-story seaside, offering four bedrooms, and two baths. A glorious outdoor kitchen, on a large sprawling stilted deck, promises to be the perfect location for food and family to celebrate. Dave emailed pictures of the attractive resort home, advising it is available the week of the fifteenth. Best of all, once Dave shared the reason for the celebration with his friend, the gentleman generously offered the use of the beach home free of charge, as an anniversary gift! Everyone should comfortably fit in this spacious beach front palace. The rooms are generous in size and capable of housing Brandon, Carrie, Dana, Ric, and baby Sydney, Kelly and I, and the Langley's who made this arrangement possible.

The month prior to embarking on our celebration, Dana and Rik looked into some of the beach activities available to the public. They suggested parasailing along the shore line. I've seen that thrilling adventure play out each time Kelly and I went to the beach. A few years ago, we considered parasailing tandem, but passed on the opportunity. Dana of course suggested she will fly solo. I suspect she will book the charter which will take her as high and fast as permissible. It sounds like great fun but at sixty-seven, keeping both feet on the ground walking the shoreline with Kelly might be a bit more appropriate. Just the same, this could be my last shot to give it a go.

Kelly and I arrived on Wednesday, a day ahead of the crowd. This gave us time to check the place out, fill the fridge and stock the cooler with cold drinks. While in town we picked up a couple of steaks worthy of a beach front anniversary grilling celebration. For some reason while shopping, Dana's suggestion of parasailing began to reclaim my attention. Dare I reconsider and entertain the opportunity to participate?

Back at the beach house, Kelly was busy in the kitchen preparing gourmet salads for our outdoor feast. I patiently watch the charcoals slowly inch their way closer and closer to arriving at the optimal gray exterior, cuing me to gently plop down our juicy handpicked entrees. Baked potatoes already prepared indoors, were waiting in the oven. This meal is the exact one we enjoyed on our first wedding anniversary. We love tradition; and our fond memories never ever get old!

With steaks on, and meat tongs in hand, I patiently wait for the ideal time to turn these beauties. While pausing, pleasing mixtures of melodic coastal sounds fill the air waves. A pleasant breeze greets my face, and gently echoes in my ears. The surf rolls recurrently in relaxing, reassuring, rhythmic, resonating refrains... couldn't resist. The happy voices of a young family splashing at the shore a couple of hundred yards down the coast, joins the harmonious audio blend. Finally, the ever-present call of the gulls, as they forage for evening dinner, completes the calming background soundtrack.

After Kelly's delicious salad, we enjoyed one mouthwatering taste satisfying bite of fillet after another, until our plates were empty. We bought fixings to make s'mores for our kids, but couldn't resist the chance to make a few, while the coals were still willing. As we enjoyed our sweet treat, the sound of a single engine plane gained our attention. As the plain neared our area, a skydiver exited the aircraft. After a few seconds of freefalling, he deployed his chute and safely landed a few hundred yards up the coast from our beachfront location. Shortly thereafter a boat pulling tandem parasailers cruised in front of our beach house, a few hundred yards from shore. We could barely hear the voices of the excited pair laughing and chatting with unbridled enthusiasm. My face lit up with the excitement of the moment. My delight did not go unnoticed by my darling wife, and after swallowing her final bit of s'more, with great conviction and direct eye contact she uttered, "Don't even think about it"! I paused and looked back at the parasailers now far down shore. I then looked back at Kelly who had not taken her eyes off of me, since issuing her decree. "What", I simply uttered knowing full well she knew I pictured myself engaging in both of those thrilling sports. "Really Dan, you've never tried either of those activities, now at close to seventy you think it time to give it a go"? My voice of reason has spoken. "Ok", I said with a clear tone of resignation. Perhaps fishing from the dock and a boat ride is a bit more my speed. I must admit, while skydiving would be exhilarating, it isn't really a sport I'd honestly consider at this point. But I can't help to think parasailing is still a possibility, even at my age. I'm only sixty-eight; and I'm not quite ready for the rocking chair by any means.

After cleanup and a restful chat in our beach chairs, the clear evening air transitioned into a sky full of stars. After identifying the few constellations which I could; (the Little Dipper still baffles me), we retired into the beach house. What a spectacular array of events I have to choose from, when journaling later this evening.

Tomorrow we will greet Dana, Rik, and baby Sydney. We learned Brandon and Carrie are bringing Carrie's younger sister Ella, who is excited to finally see the Atlantic shore line. On Friday Dave and Cindy Langley will come down to share in our celebration, and then all of us will depart sometime Saturday afternoon. But, before we are blessed with the beaming spirits of family and friends, Jesus shared these words with me tonight...

Her golden soul lays gentle and still
A spirit in tune to Father's will
Her warm heart glistens
She patiently listens
She protects and keeps me whole
Each day or in evenings chill

Caring and sure never to waver
Surrendering nothing from the heart
All others come first
In tune to her Savior
As she Imparts wisdom
Quenching my thirst

My life she'll protect
Allowing no harm
To darken my door
She'll detour and deflect
She'll dissolve and disarm
All foes which cause me harm

I awoke lying on my back and staring at the ceiling fan. I turn to the night stand and see it is 6:31 am. The dream I received last night was clear evidence I am blessed to have a living guardian angel; my wife Kelly Lynn. Over the years, Kelly has repeatable displayed one selfless act after another. She has poured her heart out to the sick and needy, sacrificed her time to counsel friends and neighbors in distress, and faithfully mentored and protected every child fortunate enough to be in her classroom. I, more than anyone, has been a recipient of her wisdom and heaven-sent guidance.

With a gently ocean breeze drifting across our bed, I turn to look at my beauty quietly resting and enjoying her remaining minutes of sleep. I gently touch her cheek producing a sweet smile indicating she is awake, but not yet willing to open her eyes, and gift me with the Webster sparkle. Minutes later she awakens. I receive a peck on the cheek and a warm smile. "I hope you dreamt about parasailing", she quipped. She then repositioned herself propping up on one elbow. With a slight turn of her head, a raised eyebrow, and I wry smile, she waited for my reply. At that point I realized dreaming was as close as I'll get to parasailing. Kelly is my in-house protector, forever wise when I am not, and my inner voice reminding me I am sixty-eight not twenty-eight. Jesus reconfirmed what I already knew; her conviction for my well-being.

Today will be a great day. We will receive family, fellowship safely and break bread with joy and happiness. I'm certain some of us will partake in the outdoor activities the beach offers, but we will choose wisely and close the day unharmed. After all, Kelly, Jesus and I look forward to celebrate our fiftieth anniversary, five years from now, in some grand way.

-The Ohio Celebration-

We've arrived in Toledo, Ohio ready to celebrate the second half of our anniversary weekend. Daryl picked us up at the airport, and we will be bunking at his house during our stay. With their kids, Laura and Freddy, moved out and starting their own families, Daryl and Sherry are empty nesters and have ample room for Kelly and me. Mom has been staying with Daryl for a couple of years. At ninety-one she is still sharp but restricted physically, and needs much assistance. Daryl and Sherry care for Mom with joyful hearts, and willingly give her the loving home she provided, when we were growing up.

The first event of our celebration will take place at Ron's house. His three girls are thirty somethings and have blessed Ron and Susie with five grandchildren. Somehow Ron managed to survive the financial and emotional joy of three country club weddings; correction one wedding took place at the Toledo Zoo. Spring, the youngest, married a fellow zoologist in front of the bear exhibit. That darling niece of ours seriously travels to the beat of her own drummer. By the way her last name is Rivers, so the water related theme continues, or shall I say *flows on*. Kelly's Dad is ninety-three and has recently moved into assisted living. Many of his friends have moved into this complex and they are keeping fit and active with swimming pool therapy, pinochle games and great fellowship. We for sure will visit him and catch up.

Back to the celebration plans, Ron and Susie have a great day planned for us. Oldest daughter Brooke is in the catering business, and owns a food vehicle, the *Boardwalk Five Star* food truck. The truck provides gourmet dining right on the customers premises. They provide tables complete with linens, appropriate place settings, and elegant table ware. Food is prepared on the truck and in the yard on portable ovens and grills. Everything from steak to lobster with gourmet sides, are prepared and served by a tuxedo garbed staff. Five-star dining in your back yard is their catch phrase. What luxury! By the way, I learned Ron has a nice comfy park bench in his garden area; I suspect Jesus and I will take a break or two during the course of the long day.

Our second day will be a day long visit to Cedar Pointe amusement part in Sandusky. Can't wait to reminisce and see how the park has evolved. This time, rather than just Kelly and me, we will bring a group of twenty or so. It's been nearly forty years since we've been there and I suspect I will hardly recognize the place. I know it has newer higher and faster steel coasters, capable of doing things we could only have dreamt about in the past. I hope to try one or two of the new coasters, but the days of 8 hours of endless coaster hopping are long gone. Even my lovely voice of reason does not have to remind me of that fact.

Day one is well underway and the food is five stars as promised. The fillets are fork tender and tasty. Lobster tails in butter sauce were the best I've eaten and the crab legs were beyond succulent. The staff is in the process of filling an eight-foot dessert table. There is a sample of just about every type of sweet treat one could imagine. While awaiting the *sugar coma of joy* to be fully displayed for our sweet tooth indulgence, a rather lively and competitive volley game in unfolding. Ron and two of his sons-in-law (the boys are on the opposite team from Ron) are engaging in some friendly G-rated trash talking.   The verbal exchange has something to do with Ron's age and the size of his belly from the sounds of the chatter.   As a result of a wager brokered during the heated contest, at games end Ron got tossed into his pool.   The two boys are Rik's size, poor Ron didn't have a chance; I thought it rather hilarious Ron got drenched in his own pool, and I couldn't stop laughing. Kelly finally suggested I curb my excitement, or I might find myself in the deep end with him. Would they dare do that to the man of the hour?   "Yes, they sure would", Susie informed me with a chuckle. "My sons in law are super guys, but when it comes to sports, they have the go for the jugular mentality". I quickly decided to quell my enthusiasm.

As the evening came to a close, the food truck cleaned up and left. We all pitched in and began returning Ron and Susie's yard back to its familiar setting. Our group was the last to leave. On the way back to Daryl and Sherry's place, Kelly asked if we could pass by our old house in Toledo. It had been years since we'd seen the place, but we accommodated Kelly's request. There it was. We pulled up on the side street and parked under Darla, the old elm tree still strong and healthy is short left field. "There's the gray monster", Kelly said recalling one of the stories I shared a few years ago. The house has been renovated and resided; no more gray asbestos shingles, thank goodness! As Kelly chatted with Daryl about some of his old memories, I pictured myself on the field and playing ball with the old gang of kids. The yard looks so tiny compared to my memories of the place. A beam cast from the streetlight indicated third base was still there. I had to touch the base just one last time. What a blessing it is to be back here. Wonderful memories of Dad are beginning to come to mind. It's been eleven years since he passed, yet standing here, his wit and wisdom remain clear as the evening air, almost as though he was still with us. I give thanks to the Lord for the blessing of having him well into adulthood.

As we left the old homestead and headed over to Daryl's, Sherry detailed the overnight accommodations with us. Given Mom has permanently moved into

Laura's room; Kelly and I will be bunking in Freddy's old room. With all of us exhausted from the long but heartwarming day, we were all ready for bed. Once hugs and good nights were exchanged, we headed upstairs. Daryl had hung a number of Mom and Dad's old family pictures along the stairway walls. Kelly and I stopped to take a look and she reminisced over some that she had recalled. When I spotted my all-time favorite baseball photo, posing with Dad and Daryl, I couldn't resist carefully taking it off the wall and bringing into the dining room. Mom, Daryl and Sherry had not yet gone to bed so I insisted all five of us take a look at the prized shot. With Mom seated at the dining room table, I placed the photo in front of her. The four of us gathered around her, pointing at the photo and commenting on our expressions, clothes, and buzz haircuts. Mom then gently touched the photo sliding her fingertips back and forth over the three of us, then paused to rest her fingers on Dad. She recalled the day and commented on our similar expressions. She remembered she said something to set the scene, but didn't recall her words. I did recall exactly what she said, and I repeated her memorable phrase word for word. She smiled and nodded her head in fond memory, as I recited her words. What a special moment. This very instant may be my fondest memory of the week. What a blessing it is to share it with this loving group.

I carefully placed the cherished photo safely back on the hook as we ascended up to bed. I believe my journal entry tonight was one of my longest ever. So many fond memories, too many to list were experienced today, each of which shared with the dearest people in my life. Freddy's old bed was only a double, but the two of us comfortably snuggled as the lights switched off. Kelly was out just as quickly as the lights were turned off. I joined her shortly after, but only after replaying several of today's memorable events in my mind. Tomorrow is another big day, and the weather is forecasted to be ideal for outdoor activities. I don't think I need Jesus to tell me to cool it on the coaster count. Kelly and I will leave that heavy load to our kids and their families.

Jesus knows how much I treasure family; His thoughts seem to mirror mine as I dozed off in his care...

No words can explain
No thoughts can express
The joy of family bonds

Not on this plane
Can I imply or impress
The love when family responds

No questions are asked
No rules are in place
No heart shall come undone

Both now and days past
In Father's true grace
United we are as one

I'll guide in My sweetness
In faith I will mentor
As true as your hearts desire

Now enter in fleetness
Left right and center
My rest you'll surely acquire

This loving message was a simple in content; nothing big or profound for me to receive and contemplate. Simply put, our family loves one another, we help each other as needed, we offer guidance when appropriate, we trust and support, and rejoice together. As we do these things in tune to God's guiding hand, out of family love. No bigger passion exists in our mortal world.

By the way, everyone survived our big day at Cedar Point. As expected, our kids and their kids ran the gamut of coaster rides, just as Kelly and I did forty-five years ago. The Jumbo Jet has since departed and is alive and well in Europe, thrilling our friends on the other side of the pond.

The Blue streak is still operational, and the two of us rekindled decades of old memories past, on that old wooden classic not once but twice. By day's end, as we strolled back to the cars, each of the younger generation fell victim to the amusement park zombie look. A dozen exhausted, weather blown, raspy voiced but grinning happy people piled in the cars to head back home. We each mustered enough energy to meet back at Ron's for ice cream and share our best stories of the day. What a blessing this entire week has been.

The entire day at the amusement park was filled with thrilling moments. Kelly and me, once again had the pleasure of enjoying our favorite coaster from our youth. But we both agreed, riding the merry-go-round with our sweet little Sydney, the same way we did with Dana, was the best memory of all. Thank you, dear Father, for allowing us to relive those wonderful blessings, and create new memories with our lovely granddaughter. Amen!

Age 69

Carson's Frist Days

2015

We celebrated Brandon's move out of our house in nineteen ninety-nine. This was perhaps the biggest step he had taken in his adult life. A step which proved to be just one of the many successful progressions, he's achieved in his business and personal life.

It is a common sentiment for most parents; to smile in admiration as their child moves out of the nest, and takes their place in the responsible world of adulthood. As we travel in faith in search of our position in God's will, each step taken contributes to our overall journey. We cherish those strides which lead to our joys and successes. But obstacles lay before us, and there are days where advancing forward in a positive manner is a challenge. Hence the term two steps forward one step back. We've all experienced ups and downs, and no one is exempt from this reality. Enjoy the positives as abundantly as possible, but make no mistake; the negatives will attempt to find us in a heartbeat, and demand our attention at every possible opportunity. So how do we turn a deaf ear to this uninvited visitor? Let's examine.

First, remember every experience, even the unpleasant ones, happen for a reason. Perhaps we were meant to gain knowledge for future experiences; enabling us to mature by enduring certain undesirable events. Perhaps we'll acquire an appreciation or strengthen ourselves by enduring a challenging time. My son Brandon is no exception when it comes to experiencing difficulties. Fortunately, his forward steps seem to advance at a higher percentage than mine, when I was his age. At least that is the impression I get from my observations.

Along those same lines, I mentioned in conversation with Kelly how Brandon seems to manage the challenges of life and take things in stride very well. Her reply was, "are you kidding"? I was a bit confused by her response. She went on about the things in his life that he regards as high priority, such as his female relationships. He has enjoyed several over the last couple of years, though all of which ended at some point. Kelly mentioned a few of the young ladies by name, and I recalled all of them as very nice girls. "Indeed, they were nice girls" Kelly agreed. But at some point, all relationships either grow and strengthen, or they recede in some way. At that juncture, people simply part company as friends or part company entirely. Perhaps they determined there were limits to their compatibility. Well, true to a point, but as Kelly put it, most of the women in Brandon's life were not thinking of motherhood as a high priority, even if marriage was in the conversation. It seems Brandon wanted to be a dad, far more than any of his female friends were willing to consider motherhood. I can understand and relate, given our Dana was much the same way. Career was first and foremost, marriage was second and then the arrival of Sydney came, once Dana was ready to become a fulltime mother. But back to Brandon.

So while good friendship remained in place with most of Brandon's female friends, his determination to embrace fatherhood, had to patiently wait. Just the same, he continued to enjoy life and wait for the fruits of God, to eventually bless him when the time is right.

At age thirty-seven, Brandon met a girl, who he would eventually marry two years later. Her name was Carrie Anne Dawkins. Carrie is the sweetest thing you'd ever want to meet. She is from Houston, TX and is a perfect example of not everything from Texas is big. Carrie is small in stature at five feet even, but a bigger and kinder heart would be difficult to find. She is a dental hygienist, and had moved to our area the year before she and Brandon met. That meeting, not surprisingly, took place in the dental chair when Brandon was in for a checkup.

At some point they started dating, then married about a year later. They started their family soon after, and our grandson Carson was born this year.

As any grandparent will tell you, each grandchild is a gift from heaven. Most of us agree, when you bring a child into the world, you realize the amazement of the gift of life. When your off spring brings a new life into the world, that joy increases exponentially.

When I first saw Carson in the hospital, I had a feeling of total connection with him. He endured a bout with Jaundice and had to stay in the hospital a few days after Carrie was discharged. Within a week he was bright eyed, attentive and ready to go home to Mom and Dad. Later that same day, after Brandon and Carrie had him settled in at home, Kelly and I stopped over for a visit. As I looked at him in his little bed, he quietly rested and occasionally opened and closed his eyes. He peacefully lay helpless and innocent as we all smiled and took him in. A couple of times though, he and I made eye contact for a brief second or two. I was warmed by his look and I felt a distinct attachment to him. Well, rightly so; we are blood relatives and he is the son of my son. Yet, in addition to being family, I felt a connection; a bond of some type, a camaraderie, something special uniting us in a unique way. I'm his grandpa and I suspect this may be easily explained as typical behavior between grandpa and grandson, but somehow a link is resonating between him and me. I can feel it.

A few days later we invited Brandon and Carrie to spend a couple of days with us. They just completed their first full week of parenthood. Kelly thought we could have them over and give them a bit of a break from their new adjustment to life in the real world. A bit of relief in the form of a staycation at our house, so they could enjoy some time together, or perhaps go out, as we took on the joy of taking care of Carson. They packed up a couple of days needs for both themselves and for Carson, and came over in time for dinner on Friday evening.

During the overnight Carrie took care of the 2:00 AM feeding as a hungry Carson awoke, breaking the stillness of our household. After he finished feeding, she put him down for the rest of the night. In the early morning Kelly and I were willing participants in answering his call shortly before six. I warmed up the bottle as Kelly gently rocked our little guy in the family room. With bottle in hand, he began taking in the formula as he rocked and slowly again begin falling into a state of quiet bliss. I had stretched out on the sectional and Kelly scooted his little bed up to the edge of the chaise where I was laying down. Kelly grabbed her phone as started to take the first of many pictures, which Carson and I would be part of. Carson was now well into newborn oblivion and I too took the opportunity to doze off.

Sometime within the next hour or so, amid the soothing silence of the early morning, a gentle rush of words gently blanketing over the shared space where Carson and I lay...

I need not rush to seek his hand
Or reach in quickness toward his arms
His nearness seeks to quell my fears
Before my worries even land

For fears are not mine to bear
No peace eludes me if I'm still
You are my rest on vigil's watch
One thought away in simple prayer

I need not rush to seek his hand
For I'm forever in his arms
He shares each breath drawn into me
As I am strengthened where I am

As I awake and think about these words, I feel two distinct impressions regarding this message. First, I feel this is me absorbed in the constant loving clutches of Jesus's presence. This is yet another example of the life long bond shared between the two of us. That feeling alone is and always will be very special. The other interesting sensation I felt, was closeness to Carson, as those gracious words we received. I mentioned I felt an awareness connecting him and me right from the beginning. Beyond the obvious bond of family there seems to be a presence or a consciousness which we already seem to enjoy. I sense a togetherness; a unity, something which gives me the feeling we are as one, in some special way.

Who knows? Perhaps again, it is just the wishful thinking of a new grandpa, hoping he will be a special person in his new grandson's life. It may be no more than that, but my inner core is telling me there will be much to be discovered, in our new relationship. Our spirits are already soaring together; our souls are comfortable and compatible with one another, and our hearts are beating in cadence to the same drummer.

Perhaps at this point I can only say this is a *God thing* happening to me and Carson. I don't quite know. I do know, that little boy that precious creation, is going to be special and embrace the will of God in a marvelous way. I can just feel it!

Age 70

Generation to Generation

2017

Each time I see my grandchildren approach me with anticipated joy, I drop to one knee. I do so in an effort to steady myself for the onslaught of charging children, with arms extended intent on delivering a loving hug. My granddaughter Sydney is nearly four years old and possesses every bit as much energy and desire as Dana. Carson, is over a year and a half and rushes with the same loving G force. I dearly adore these two spirited creations, in ways only a grandparent can understand.

Whenever our family gathers together on a weekend or over a holiday, we celebrate in recognition of three generations of Webster / Lowe lineage. Inevitably, at some point during our family fellowship, the girls engage in discussion covering careers, homes, and certainly the children. This cues us guys to take it out on the patio and either talk sports or toss a ball around in the yard. Carson needs no encouragement to watch his dad and uncle Ric toss a ball back and forth. The guys enjoy seeing Carson develop his skills, and gently play catch with the young addition to the Lowe family. As the game draws to a close, Brandon and Ric often go into the family room and chat over a cold beverage. This creates a perfect opportunity for Carson and Grampa to bond and talk.

Carson and I have enjoyed some very interesting and stimulating *conversations*. He does most of the talking, the majority relating to the toys and trucks which he brings on every visit. A near two-year-old explains things with verve and intensity, in one riveting talking point after another. Given the significance of his disclosure, I give full attention to every detail. He studies my face as I listen, while anticipating my response. Typically, my remarks go no deeper than commenting on the color or size of the toy, but he revels in our exchange. He maintains an inquisitive look throughout our conversation. For seconds at a time he will study my face in deep thought, then resurface sweet and carefree as can be. Eventually he will exit the scene in search of his dad and uncle. Soon Brandon and Carson will reunite, with the end result culminating into a tickle Carson's belly party on the family room floor. Uncle Ric, given his six four two forty stature, often picks Carson up elevating him high into the air; then flies him around the house, like a Navy jet soaring from room to room, (sound effects courtesy of Uncle Ric of course).

Days like these are common place, but very special. Our family bond again strengthens and grows with each gathering. Much of that growth, as Kelly and I have discovered, has occurred in our kids and their spouses. Their young children have become catalysts in their relationships. Dana and Ric are still young. The presence of Sydney seems to temper their professional drive, to make certain the Webster/Lowe *family first* mantra is not forgotten. My little darling of a granddaughter already seems to possess many of Kelly's traits; she's already a voice of reason. The other day Dana was commiseration about the weeds in her garden. Despite weeding by hand and spraying, she was getting a bit in the flesh regarding her losing battle with these unwanted invaders. Sydney interceded to gently calm and comfort her mother. "Syd, you sound exactly like your gramma", Dana said hugging her daughter, while inviting Kelly in for a group embrace. Just like her gramma I thought. Somewhere there is a lucky little boy, who will be blessed with a *jewel of a bride* someday; just as I was.

Similarly, Brandon has continued to develop into a thankful and humble young man. I think his kind nature and patient heart play key elements in his growth. Carrie came into his life and though they dated for just a few months, he knew in his heart of hearts, Carrie was the one. Once they were blessed with a son, Brandon's faith soared. That miracle from God was life changing for both Carrie and my son. Sometime after Brandon became a father, he coined the term "nugget of clarity". These are the experiences one receives when spiritually growing or when a great understanding is received. It's a time when Jesus makes something perfectly clear, and one is better for it. The birth of his child, for example, brought new responsibilities as both a parent and husband. Brandon said a *nugget of clarity* was received during that process. He simply adores that son of his and the two of them are practically inseparable.

Today we were again blessed with a visit from our kids and grandchildren. Each time they visit, the grandkids appear to be growing faster than the weeds in Dana's garden. They jump from one clothes size to the next seemly overnight. I only hope their love for the Lord grow as quickly.

After today's heart soothing visit came to an end, Kelly and I reflect on the precious time our family spent together. Sydney is an engineer in the making and Carson's desire to keenly seek answers for his curious mind brings huge smiles to us both. Our list of blessings and words of thanks to Jesus for the jubilance He has placed in our lives could go on till morning. But His only longing is to hear we love Him, and to love those who grace our day.

After prayers, I lay in bed a bit worn from the day, but peaceably relaxed and quickly drop off into dreamland. I am sitting amidst a complete hush; no sound challenges the stillness. I sit in revitalizing repose, resting, relaxing, refreshing and reinvigorating; reclined on a park bench. I am resolved in purposeful peace, or should I say resolved in resolute reconciliation. Around me is the near silent flutter of golden red leaves gently dropping from the branches overhead. I don't see Carson, but I sense he is near. I hear Sydney playing in the distance; perhaps we are at the park? The spirited words of Jesus describe the moment...

No finer gift than our young
Inventive, bold, your heart they hold
You flourish when you are among
The words they speak
The songs they've sung
And stories yet untold

Falling and drifting from above
In silent hush upon the ground
Golden leaves rest all around
Subdued and patient by God's will
All thoughts are safe and sound

Are these Your words or not at all?
Or convictions felt as children call?
The leaves in motion bare a notion
Though not sure what at all

Could be just a peaceful dawn
Perhaps that's what this is
But thoughts now spawn as I've been drawn
To think these words are his

Opening my eyes, I discover the new day I still arriving. A peaceful dawn, not unlike the one I just dreamt, will soon bloom into a glorious bright fall morning. I look toward Kelly, and quickly realize she is far from starting her new day. We are in the loving arms of a pleasant autumn morning, soon to reveal its striking bright colors upon first light. My just received dream revealed no sound other than the reassuring near silent flutter of leaves landing around me. It is unclear if my spirit laden thoughts depicted me as the topic or someone else, since the inspirational presence of others surrounded me. A relaxing smile engulfs my face, as I ponder the feelings and impressions of last night. Despite my uncertainty, I remain thankful I have again been graced with spirited guidance. In time, I know the full meaning of the message will be understood.

As the morning unfolded, Kelly asked me to take her to a couple of home I centers. It seems we are in the market for new lamps in the guest room. To our shopping list I added an item long overdue to adorn our back yard. In all these years of receiving the precious inspirations of Jesus, I have yet to feature an inviting park bench in our outdoor seating. That lovely and soothing feature will soon be ours.

Heading out to shop, I pause and look forward with great anticipation to the first time Jesus and I relax in the tranquility of our yard, and quietly chill while talking about the first thing which comes to mind.

As I enter the store, being a purist, I think a traditional wooden park bench like the one I sat on so many times as a child, may be the best choice. I foresee many relaxing conversations and good times with Carson and Sydney in our future. But given I'm older and want to share the bench with my grandkids, perhaps a swinging bench may be more to their liking, and my comfort.

Later that evening, after grilling some delicious sward fish steaks, picked up on the way home from our shopping junket, we were elbow deep in assembling our bench. In no time the final screws were tightened on my instruction free assembly. Why is it men rebuff the opportunity to follow written assembly instructions?

As I worked, Brandon and Ric assisted in setting the frame in concrete and graveling the pit. Of course, the wood is unpainted, and I'm debating on either the traditional park bench green, or possibly going with a clear lacquer coat. No time for brain testing decisions now, it's time to assist my crew so we can enjoy this baby as soon as the concrete cures. Thank you, Jesus, for your guiding skills and for keeping us company during our building session.

The following Saturday I was treated to an impromptu visit from Brandon, Carrie and Carson. On the way over to our house, Brandon asked if Carson could visit for a couple of hours. He and Carrie were asked by friends for the use of their truck, to pick up a large chest purchased on line. The chest was in the next town, and their friends offered to treat them to dinner, while they were out as their thank you for their assistance. This meant we had the pleasure of having Carson visit for at least a couple of hours, during the late fall afternoon.

The pleasing late October weather is still offering temperatures in the low seventies. Golden, crimson, and bright yellow leaves dashed through the yard, as each refreshing gust of breeze drifts across our faces. Our yard was enjoying one of God's most lovely gifts; the peak color season. After a rousing playing session on the patio, Carson and I paused for a break on our swinging bench. We comfortably settled in as Carson *scooched* in close to me; two buddies nearly seventy years in age difference, but as contented and alike in soul and spirit as two beings can be.

After a few minutes of sitting in the quiet of the afternoon, watching the leaves flutter and the occasional bird land then fly off, Carson softly said. "I love you too Grampa"? Not hearing anything specifically other than the restful autumn sounds, I wonder what Carson actually heard? *I love you too* sounds like a response to someone saying I love you. Within seconds I went back in time to my wedding day when I felt nervous, as my heart beat a mile a minute. I recall the restful look on Kelly's face as she softly said *I love you*, while escorted down the aisle by her dad. That action was followed with a quick reassurance from Jesus ….

I love you too

That moment was fifty years ago, yet it popped into my head as though a clue to a puzzle or a disclosure of some kind.

We sat there for several more minutes enjoying the breezy afternoon.   Me, Carson, and Jesus swaying together, until the temperatures dipped low enough to take our fellowship indoors. We didn't speak much after our *I love you too* discussion, but I have the feeling Carson's young mind was reeling in spiritual conversation, as was mine.

Age 71

Hearing Jesus Again

for the First Time

2018

It is an amazing experience to watch a small child observe the fascinations of life. Once they become aware of their five basic senses, they begin to discover the potential of those individual abilities. Life becomes enriched as they mature in awe of what the world has in store for them. Their priceless expressions are beautiful to witness, as they discover one new sensation after another. Eye movement, arm gestures, facial expressions and shrieks of joy, all serve as confirmation much is being processed in this young and eager spirit.

I'm of the opinion these movements are more than just the reaction of a young creation learning to manipulate a physical response in a newly discovered body. We're speaking about a new creation, with no filters yet formed, and no personal ideals yet cast; a clean sheet of paper, in need of care and guidance, and eager to journal a new life. I would suggest these young beings are already hearing the voices of guidance and receiving early tutelage from a spiritual presence, as they physically respond to those calls. Perhaps it is the early encounters of our guardian angel, eager to fellowship with their new charge? Possibly this young soul is responding to the heavenly harmonies of angels in concert? Perhaps the voice of Jesus, is offering loving words of inspiration to His young brethren? I am going to take the road of equal opportunity and suggest it is "D", all of the above.

Let's take it back a few steps; long before the above-mentioned spiritual guidance was received during our early days. The Lord created a plan for each of us, even before we were knit in mother's womb. I believe God's nurturing guidance and love, was bestowed on to us long before we took our first breath! I'm convinced I heard from Dana's daughter Sydney, during her pregnancy. I believe the Lord was already at work, imparting gifts of knowledge and bearing onto her. His guidance continues to be conveyed throughout our lives, and we will greatly benefit from His shepherding advice. In our fallen world, our resources alone are not nearly enough.

Try to think back to your earliest memory. For many it is a difficult to definitively pin point that moment, unless it is attached to a particular event. Kindergarten is an exact recollection, since it can be related to a time, a place and to a specific group of people. But clear memories prior to age five are a bit more difficult to recall, with any measurable detail. Our first four years of life are basically lost in a historical vacuum, with only few fragmented memories able to come to mind. For the most part, the first few years of our lives are left to the recollection of those who cared for us during our formative years. Jesus touched their hands, as they taught and guided us in spirit and body. Their efforts and our achievements culminate into the unforgettable stories, which become shared by family over the years to follow. One of these memorable stories was the first time I played a simple game of catch with my dad.

The game basically consisted of me and Dad, rolling a ball back and forth to one another. I have no recollection of this event, other than hearing my dad speak fondly about the joys of that day. I was one year old, perhaps a little older, and the details of the game were shared solely from his perspective. As I got older, the story gradually faded, and like so many of those early day happenings, it deeply descended into the memory abyss. Nevertheless, those early activities dutifully contribute to our make-up. Our early experiences become part of our quest to find our place in God's Plan. While that first game of catch went into hiatus for decades, a glimmer of remembrance began to come to mind, as I played a similar game with my grandson Carson.

The entire family was at Brandon's house, celebrating Carrie's birthday. Dana, Ric and Sydney were the last to arrive, and I immediately received a huge hug from Sydney as they entered. Carson and I were on the family room floor, playing amid a sea of toys, which had encircled us in every direction. I then cleared the area between him and me, and began rolling a small toy truck back and forth. Sydney scooched next to me, and looked on in delight of Carson's participation. After the truck traveled back and forth a few times, I recalled Dad's story about he and I doing something similar with a ball. I asked Brandon if he had a toy ball in the house. A small rubber ball was tossed into the room and immediately, like a blast from the past, a glimmer of my first game of catch, *some 70 years earlier,* began to surface from the afore mentioned memory abyss.

As Carson and I roll the ball back and forth, I began sensing my emotions and visions, from back in the late forties. A warm silence consumes our play area, bringing clarity and understanding, as the presence of Jesus encompasses our space. Then came these words; reassuring and filled with kindness.

The simplicity of rolling a ball
You to me, I to you
Roll back and forth this day recall
As words exchanged were few

Our gaze affixed on rolling sphere
Engrossed by this you were
Your mind in tune with eyes so clear
As tiny hands work swift and sure

Thy spirit free in two hand grasp
By young decree No boundaries cast
You changed the rule in one quick toss
Fed by the fuel Of lines to cross

A gentle flip from your hand
A one hop bounce chest high
The game enhanced by the demand
To catch it on the fly

A scream of joy
As arms up stretch
You tossed that toy
To Dad to catch
And as he did
He bounced it back

To you he did
Your eyes now gazed
In game amid
And hearts amazed

Then as the ball
Touched your hands
You will recall
It safely lands

With joyful thoughts of Dad filling my soul, I played catch with Carson while Brandon and family observed. Four generations of Lowe's became tightly united in one loving fellowship. This amazing family event is amongst the most incredible happenings I have ever been blessed to enjoy.

I am totally confident the words I just heard, are the same words I was too young to received and understand back in the late forties, as I played catch with Dad on that memorable day seventy years ago! Best of all, Jesus's depiction of the event between Carson and me, was exactly as Dad described our story so many times, so long ago.

Once the game came to an end, family members cheered for Carson and began to disperse and focus attention back on Carrie's celebration. Still seated on the floor, I took in a deep breath and continued to absorb this amazing moment. Seconds later, something remarkable and equally astonishing happened! Prior to joining the family in the next room, my darling granddaughter slid over to my side, gently touched my cheek, then unexpectedly whispered these words; "Carson heard Him too".

Age 72

Daniel's Closing Thoughts

2019

My life has been graced in a special and unique manner. I reflect in fond memory over the past seventy-two years, and give thanks to Jesus for each of those wonderful days.

Though I have been referred to as a wordsmith, I am at a loss to describe the impact of the companionship Jesus and I have shared. His guidance and encouragement have inspired me to keep my head up under any circumstance. When traveling in His light, all challenges can be faced. When I step ahead of Him, I sense uncertainty as I trek. Thankfully, His presence and guidance, is free for the asking.

While I have been gifted many memorable and touching moments as a man, my mortal life is only a tiny fraction of the elation to come; and the jubilation and reunion which the Lord and I will enjoy. The blessing and promise of eternity in the arms of Jesus, as I reunite with friends and loved ones from earlier days, will be forever ours to relish.

It is exciting to speculate what has been prepared for us. Imagine our magnificent home of countless breathtaking views, fragrant aromas, and welcoming soothing chorales arranged in perfection for our eternal awe! Rejoice, in levels of unimaginable cheer, will be everywhere. Our flaws of the past; cleansed and forgotten, Heavenly righteousness will be for all to share.

As I reflect back to my fondest thoughts, my love and appreciation for family is foremost in my heart. The guidance and life lessons I've learned from Mom, Dad, and Daryl have shaped me into the man I am today. The blessing of my dear wife Kelly and the joys we have shared together is impossible to measure. Our children, and our grandson and granddaughter, are gifts of perfection, placed in our lives simply to demonstrate the endless love God has for us.

In a final thought; and one of curiosity, I wonder if our Lord will choose a unique way to communicate and mentor Sydney and Carson, as He did for me? It would appear He already *has their ear!* One thing is certain; I cannot wait to find out how He guides each one of them.

Thank You Father, for the gift of these precious children.

Sincerely,

Daniel Ethan Lowe

Going forward from the author...

Throughout this book, the Lord's love and fondness for all of His children, was repeatedly demonstrated. His desire to mentor and guide Daniel, and all the characters in every situation, is a blessing of unparalleled measure.

Many wonderful and interesting personalities have been introduced over the first two books in this series. Each character played a vital role in their relationship with Daniel, and his magnificent gift of poetic guidance. That would be to say...

Collectively, carefully crafted characters continually cultivated crowning crescendos, creating cherished cheer... I tried to save my best alliteration for last.

As soon to be released chapters will show, Jesus's love for us is never ending, and His mentoring is always available. The detail behind all of the blessings Jesus offers the Lowe and Webster clans is incredibly wonderful, yet simplistic.

What does all that mean? Enjoy *"Nuggets of Clarity"*, and discover for yourself!

Blessings, Mike Steffke

Previous Published Works

Through My Faith Came His Words... *so I picked up a pencil and started to write...*

A series of single-word titled poems, penned through the inspirations I have received from our Lord and Savior Jesus Christ. Hope, Comfort, Freedom, Patience, and Trust are a few examples of some of the topics I chose to expound upon, and share with you in verse.

ISBN 978162523798
Xulon Press   May 2014

I Finally Came to My Senses (all five of them)

Insightful and stirring, my second book is a series of devotional poems, relaxing stories, and inspirational thoughts, regarding our sense of sight, touch, taste, hearing and smell. Utilize these wonderful tools, and waste none of the minutes, which you have been gifted. Use your God given senses (all five of them) and fully embrace the precious gift of life.

ISBN 9780999756003
Createspace   April 2018

Out of the Blue and Into My Heart   The First Forty years

This offering is the first in an exciting series about a man named Daniel Ethan Lowe. Throughout his life, Daniel has embraced the loving and guiding words of our Lord and Savior Jesus Christ, placed gently on his heart. However, Daniel receives the blessing of these shepherding words in a very unique way; Jesus speaks to him in guiding poetic verses!   Learn how the Lord's thought-provoking words inspire Daniel to live life to the fullest.

ISBN 9780999756027
Kindle Direct Publishing August 2019

www.ingramcontent.com/pod-product-compliance
Lightning Source LLC
Chambersburg PA
CBHW031953040426
42448CB00006B/337